The Evil American Empire

William D. Hindie

Rutledge Books, Inc.   Bethel, CT

Riverside Community College
Library
'98
DEC
4800 Magnolia Avenue
Riverside, CA 92506

E 840 .H53 1997

Hindie, William D.

The evil American empire

Copyright© 1997 by William D. Hindie

ALL RIGHTS RESERVED

Rutledge Books, Inc.
8 F.J. Clarke Circle, Bethel, CT 06801
1-800-278-8533

Manufactured in the United States of America

Cataloging in Publication Data
Hindie, William Davis
    The American evil empire / William D. Hindie
       p. cm.
    ISBN 1-887750-59-2
    1. Liberalism-United States. 2. Social Values-United States.
3. United States-Social conditions-1980-

306.73   97-66790

Greatness is seen in many men and women, but seldom in those whose names are plastered on too many walls.

Dedication

In Memory of my Mother.

I was born in Egypt, but my mother was all American. She taught the poor women of Egypt about freedom and democracy, and they loved her for that. Unfortunately, when I came to the United States, I found there more of a love of the God Almighty Dollar and its evil imperialism, than any search and devotion to freedom and democracy. History lies and hurts, because man is so much an actor, that he shies away from the truth, and hardly ever fully recognizes it.

This book is also dedicated to the late Clinton Rossiter, professor at Cornell and Cambridge Universities, and considered a guru of the conservative tradition in American political life.

Contents

Prologue

A new American empire certainly exists, and just like all the other empires before it in human history, the American empire has its own peculiarities, working against political freedom, democracy, and human progress.

The United States has taken on its role of world leadership, chief international bully and policeman, without having the necessary intelligence in its political establishment to protect its historical development of political freedom and democracy.

The conclusion of many American voters' surveys in 1996, was that most Americans would have rather voted for a chimpanzee than for either one of the major presidential political party candidates.

Less and less Americans were voting at all in presidential elections, and to add insult to injury, they were being told that their individual votes did not always count necessarily, because they could possibly be surpassed by the rather mysterious electoral college.

Modern man, just like the men who preceded him, is still mired in the same old deceits of human history, economics, politics, and religion.

The Cold War, just like all wars before it, was forever stupid, and one of the most costly and disastrous in human history. Unfortunately for humans, great victories for a few, nearly always come at the expense of great misery for many more.

Living in simple peace and harmony has never been a very frequent human achievement. For modern man, as in the past, the continuous pathology of political human leadership forbids it. As always for political man, power corrupts one and all, and too much power for any one man corrupts even more.

The President of the United States of America, just like most of the world's political leaders of the past, shines more often in disgrace than in any great deed or honor.

Political man is the greatest of human hypocrites and cowards, for he will hold hands with anyone; commerce, science, technology, or the military, to gain, hold, or increase his power. His best self-interest seems to be in the delay of human progress and democracy so he can retain his power.

The path of human political freedom and democracy is not as complicated as the dishonest, entrenched, elite politicians and economists of the new world order of globalization, pretend.

The path of democracy and social justice is as clear as the determination of the human political and commercial exploiters to prevent them. Fortunately for man, human progress seems to have a life of its own.

The great new wealth, produced by modern science and technology, has been used more often by the elite modern human exploiters to further enslave man, rather than to liberate him to a higher quality to his life.

An exaggerated idolatry of modern science and technology can reduce the quality of human life and the individual, rather than to improve them. In the United States alone, the quality of human life has been cut in half, between the golden 1960s and 1996.

Man has a long tragic history of abandoning common sense at the wrong time in his human progress and development. He prefers to gloat over dubious physical achievements, usually in science and technology, that hinders further social progress but flatters his tremendous ego.

A national outrage has developed in the United States in its fast growing inegalitarian society.

The American elite and the super rich are openly extorting the wealth of the nation by demanding extraordinary compensations and privileges, while bragging that only the dummies among them ever pay their fair share of income and property taxes.

The best kept secret in American government is that the cost of the welfare programs for the elite, the huge corporations, and the super rich, exceeds by far the cost of all the welfare programs for the poor and the destitute.

The modern American politicians, including the president of the nation, have become bootlickers of the special interests of the elite rich and the powerful, rather than serious societal leaders, dedicated public servants, or efficient government administrators.

The curse of modern man's intelligentsia and his elite is the same as in the past. They want extraordinary compensation, recognition, fame, and glory, without any serious commitment and dedication on their part to human progress and the common good. The tragic result for the United States of America is that their elite is by far the most costly in the world.

The trouble with most men who reach too greedily for fame, recognition, and glory is that if they ever achieve the selfish goals, they tend too easily to become ruthless human exploiters, rather than sincere contributors to human progress and the common good.

A completely unbridled American Empire could very easily become, just another Evil Empire.

Entering the 21st Century

As man gloats over all his material and scientific achievements while he prepares to enter into the 21st century, he forgets too easily his horrendous failures. Materialism has always been very important to man in its power of controlling both his mind and his body, but that power was minimized by man's slow scientific and technological progress. This gave man the time to pursue much more important intellectual and spiritual growth. It is man's intellectual growth that has guided him up the chart of human progress toward political freedom and democracy.

Materialism has always had the power to deter man's intellectual and spiritual growth and halt just about all his most valiant efforts at human progress, depending upon how intelligently he uses his knowledge of it. When his knowledge of science and technology grows too rapidly before he can assimilate intelligently their impact on his life, he usually heads straight into mayhem and disaster.

Human progress has always had a life of its own with steps forward and backward, depending very much on man's intelligent use of his science and technology which become main building blocks of his materialism. Intelligent economic priorities thus

1

allow man his aspirations for human progress. Political freedom, democracy, equal opportunity, and an equitable egalitarian society are important goals of his search for human progress. Materialism can thus be used to forward or retard human progress and man's history is mostly tragic because he has failed to use it properly and intelligently for progress.

Modern man parades too proudly his scientific and technological achievements, far ahead of any spiritual and intellectual growth. He is far too eager to brag about sometimes absurd and wasteful new technologies than he is to demonstrate progress in the search for a higher quality of human life.

Modern man likes to forget his barbaric rampages of genocide, political violence, and economic greed that marked his 20th century as one of the most violent and destructive in his history. He tries to deny that modern science and technology have completely failed to produce true viable human progress.

Modern man's destructive cultural absurdity in the 20th century has reached such a negative point of no return that he ought to question his complete absence of true pragmatic intelligence, instead of continuing his mad addiction for even more fickle scientific knowledge.

Man's intellectual growth has suffered a terrible setback with the invention of his computer machines and their artificial intelligence. Man's modern computation machines have only increased the speed, and thus the potential, of man's forever long-lasting history of abuse and self-destruction.

Modern man has become so dependent upon forever increasing his scientific knowledge and creating new technologies that he hardly bothers to judge them intelligently, according to their true pragmatic values. Modern man's huge unlimited ego has gotten in the way of his common sense, and too many of his new technologies have backfired to do him more harm than any possible good. Modern man's addiction to materialism and self-abuse makes him more absurd than most animals.

Already, millions of humans have been sacrificed, killed, or maimed by modern man's machines in wars, industrial accidents, and ecological disasters. Many of modern man's most celebrated machines, such as the common automobile, have turned against him to do him more harm than good. Even so, modern man has never shown the courage to completely discontinue the machines that he knows do him harm. Sadly, many of the machines that modern man has become addicted to were invented in searching for weapons of war. It is not surprising then that modern man is a very poor judge of the true values of his new machines and technologies, and he gives far too much recognition and social status to science and technology at the expense of his health, happiness, and common sense.

Modern man has not cured himself from his long history of prejudice, jealousy, genocide, violence, and greed. His new science makes him more dangerous to himself and all other life forms upon his planet and in outer space. The bicycle, not his more exotic machines, may be his most intelligent one, because it simply has done him far less harm. The poor and the hungry may have done man less harm than the rich and the powerful who have used science more for economic exploitation and greed than for human progress. The danger is real and the evidence is stark that modern man is stupid enough to abuse the use of his machines and that he has fallen into an ominous idolatry of science and technology.

After one of the most ironic industrial accidents in Chernobyl, the whole superpower of the former Soviet Union fell apart and disintegrated.

The Soviet Union sometimes claimed that it was a socialist republic and sometimes it was a communist one, but all along it was nothing more than just another cruel military dictatorship. Just like modern man, the Soviet Union lied and deceived itself. Too much power corrupts one and all and the Soviet Union was not the first and probably not the last Evil Empire. All superpowers are potential evil empires and that is why the United Nations was born. But it too can fail in its task, because it is saddled with the same sick pathology of human leadership that has ruled most of the world since the dawn of history.

Modern man should look at all the obvious reasons why the mad Soviet dictatorship crumbled so rapidly. Many of those reasons are so obvious that hey tend to be quickly forgotten, while others are more subtle and subject to debate. The former Evil Empire was bitten by all the consuming fires that kill and destroy all chances of democracy: prejudice, nationalism, ethnic jealousy, military imperialism, all out competition, winning at all cost, and last but not least, greedy consumption and destruction of it's empire's natural resources. Its false set of economic priorities and its expensive military imperialism caused its own demise. It simply followed the course of most other cruel dictatorships until it destroyed itself. Other dictatorships should be fairly warned but will probably remain just as blind.

As modern man prepares to enter into the 21st century, he may be heading toward some more tragic misery of his own making. History shows how often the elite leadership of man miscalculates and leads him backward instead of forward. Human intelligence grows slower than science and technology.

History shows how many great powers have come and gone, with only a very small fraction of their populations, ever rising much above the enslavement level. Even after the great industrial revolution and the huge development of modern science and technology in the 20th century, the quality of human life did not improve for a huge segment of the human race, worldwide.

Modern man appeared not much different than his predecessors in catering more to his vices than his virtues. His uniquely sedentary life of machines, computers, physical ease, ostentation, and self-gratification tended to be mind-shrinking rather than stimulating any new horizons of human progress and intelligence.

The obsession with science and technology and the rise of awesome destructive military power had created a new elite, perfectly disposed toward the exploitation of the rest of the human race. The prospects of a democratic egalitarian society faded drastically with the creation of a very closed-minded new elite. Poverty and starvation were becoming more widespread than at any time in previous human history, in spite of the great wealth of a few nations. Science and technology were being used for military, economic, and political imperialism, rather than for human progress and democracy. Globalization of the world's economy was becoming known as the revolution of the elite, with the destruction of small free enterprise, labor, the middle class, and egalitarian social justice around the world.

On the approach of the 21st century, the United States of America, as one of the last remaining superpowers, bore a tremendous responsibility for the future of the entire human race.

A Fool's Paradise

According to Webster's dictionary, a fool is a person lacking in judgment and prudence, or a retainer formerly kept in great households to provide casual entertainment, and commonly dressed in motley, with caps, bells, and baubles. A fool can also be victimized and made to appear foolish. He can be a harmlessly deranged person, lacking in common powers of understanding. A fool can be imitated or he can try to imitate another fool. A fool can be someone with too much appetite or some other form of self-gratification he cannot control. According to some philosophers, most men are fools, but the qualifications are peculiarly fitting to historians and politicians.

Human history is nothing more than a tragic and erratic tale of the ship of fools that forms most of the human race, creating its own storms and shipwrecks. There is no greater fool than an overeducated fool. Many of the ancient historians served as court jesters, entertainers, and teachers in the courts of kings and tyrants. They developed the lies and myths of history in praise of their masters. Some became skilled poets and artists in creating their legends of eulogy, but others sometimes became jealous of their masters and lusted for power. Some plotted against their masters and sometimes succeeded in overthrowing them. Too much power corrupts one and all.

A fool, just like any other simple primate, falls in love easily with any power he can muster and command, no matter how basic and humble that power may be. It is nearly a rule of life that there is some basic power in its existence. Different forms of life demand different forms of power. Life thrives only with the use of intelligent power, but too many men strive too much for unreasonable and destructive powers.

A fool's paradise is where a fool prospers more than an honest man. Man has an uncanny knack from the beginning of his history of creating an unending series of his fool's paradises that he has the gall to pass off as noble and viable societies of men. Whereas once there was only the historians and the court jesters who could pass on the news of man's fool's paradise, with the help of science and technology in modern times, the mass media rises devotedly to accelerate the spread of man's fool's paradise to every corner of the world. The historians, the politicians, and the mass media practically dictate and control modern man in every sense of the word, as he has never been controlled before in all of his history.

The modern mass media, driven principally by its thirst for political and commercial powers, thrives upon sensationalism and all of man's other vices. Its great devotion to the commercial profit motive assures its dedication to all the negatives of human vices rather than to anything positive in human virtues. The modern mass media continuously flatters the club of fools that has helped create an impossible and self-destructive modern style to human life. It is as if modern science and technology have helped create social havoc around the world, with all the greed and violence of a Dantean *Inferno* or some other fool's paradise.

With so much concentration on the negatives in the human psyche, it is a miracle that anything positive can ever be reported in the mass media. The modern mass media is particularly dominating in a superpower like the United States, where it is permitted to be monopolized by big business. It is a rule that squelches a variety of intellectual thought, that is so necessary to the development of any democracy.

When national economies were not as well developed, the elite ruling class that existed still remained productive and self-supporting. But after the great industrial revolution, there was a huge increase in the number if bureaucrats, technocrats, corporate enterprise managers, and government officials forming a new ruling class nearly totally out of control and mostly neither productive, self-supporting, or accountable.

In primitive economies, the chieftain took full responsibility for clothing, feeding, and housing all his constituents. Skill, responsibility and self-sacrifice were required of the chief or his tribe would perish. The prosperity of the tribe depended upon the wisdom of the chief, and if he failed or burned out, he was quickly replaced. None of this personal responsibility or accountability exists in the forever growing, out of control, ruling class of modern man.

Democracy depends very heavily upon a fair and equitable egalitarian society, with equal opportunity and education for all. An advanced developed industrialized economy, subject to the constant changes in scientific and technological knowledge, can easily strain all the most essential principles of a democracy. Ironically, new knowledge can cause a new upheaval and destruction of an obsolete old industry, creating new social and economic distress and injustice. Education and wise economic planning are essential to protect democracy and social justice from these potentially traumatic upheavals.

The rapid advance in modern science and technology in the 20th century has already proven to have been of very mixed blessings. Modern science and technology can kill and destroy, just as easily as it can build and benefit.

Man will be never be able to progress properly until he refuses to settle disputes and arguments by physical force. Many of the greatest statesmen of man have expressed that same opinion. But ironically, modern man in the 20th century increases tenfold nearly all levels of his violence. It is as if his great scientific and technological advances have been misdirected and misused for this negative purpose. Modern nations have kept huge standing armies at a huge expense to their progress, even in peacetime. The temptation to use such armies resulted in innumerable and senseless wars during the century, proving that man produces most of his own misery.

At the beginning of human history, leadership was essential and man was forced to respect authority or else he had to leave his family or tribe and survive on his own. Man was always a jealous animal though, and often a fool, so that he would kill his brother or sister to steal or gain power. Human leadership remained mostly in the hands of a single strong individual, until complicated modern civilizations developed with a forever larger ruling clique. Violence thrived in man's pursuit of power. His worst enemy was his own weak and violent character.

Man often declares himself to be a social animal and when he lives peacefully in his family, he is subjected to his first political experience. Socialism is the political ideal of the human family, where every individual is supposed to reach his greatest potential—sometimes at the expense of other members of the family. Socialism is the best development of the individual in the family with the help and self-sacrifice of the whole family. The good health of a human family depends greatly on the quality and good character of its leadership. Unfortunately, the human family is rarely ideal.

Modern science and technology in advanced industrialized nations, create countless complicated interdependent bureaucracies, leading to political chaos and false economic priorities, while losing sight of all the goals of democracy. Countless bureaucracies lead to countless clubs of fools with only their own interests at heart at the expense of freedom and democracy in the rest of the nation. The politically independent free-loving individual, who represents the vast majority of the people in a democracy, finds himself completely overlooked by his nation's economic and political system.

The only way democracy can work is to honor all work equally and equitably. Some reasonable principles of an egalitarian value system have to be implemented, and that necessitates some degree of all out socialism. Under true democratic principles, a meritorious street cleaner should be recognized more by society, than a corrupt and incompetent manager of either the private or the public sector.

Man has no problems in devising just theories and guides to honorable behavior, but he does have a tremendous problem with his honesty—in doing as he preaches. Man may be a social animal and claim that he loves democracy, but he is also a most corrupt hypocrite, never loving democracy as much as he claims. Man, the most corrupt animal, competes for power and recognition at the expense and the reputation of his fellow man.

It is man's dishonesty and bad character that makes government necessary, with laws to punish completely outlandish violent and criminal behavior. Man searches for leadership, but he finds nearly none.

Equal social status and justice in the workplace should not interfere with the chain of command, the cohesion and the productivity in the common effort. But man is a big hypocrite and his bad character makes him nearly always hate democracy, no matter what he pretends, so that he creates his own problems.

Man competes for leadership, but unfortunately the first lesson

11

he learns in the corruption of his society is that the leader of his pack is usually the most ignominious and perverted.

Man has always been quite aggressive and perverted, and has made a great mess out of his competitions. Animals compete, so do men, and so do many living plants. The question, so ignored remains: "Are not men supposed to be more intelligent than plants and animals?" Where are all the benefits to man's mad love affair with competition? Have not nearly all the greatest works in human culture been produced by the great masters who absolutely refused to compete against anyone else but themselves?

Modern man creates his fool's paradise in his mindless competition and his pursuit of greed and the profit motive. He claims that competition produces quality, while all too often it does the exact opposite.

The former Evil Empire, the Soviet Union, fell apart in its mindless competition with the West in this pursuit of power, consumption, and greed, ending in the ecological catastrophe of Chernobyl.

Modern man's fool's paradise is to consume until he is consumed. He threatens all life upon earth until his unlimited greed moves him to outer space.

All the folly of modern man in the 20th century was fully exposed by the war in Bosnia. During all the genocide, the rape, the senseless murder, and destruction not a single area of human leadership and authority—national or international—proved itself forthright and honorable enough to stop the mayhem in time. The United Nations, the North Atlantic Treaty Organization, the United States, the Soviet Union, the three major religions involved with their pompous popes—nothing stopped modern man's false priorities and human folly.

Modern man's fool's paradise comprised his nationalism, his

religions, his ethnic folly, his corrupt character, and practically all his political and economic priorities. In a simple single nutshell, the Bosnian War atrocities proved the greatest lesson gathered from history; that human leadership is mostly absent and a mirage. Worst of all, both the United States and the Soviet Union chose to continue their exploration of outer space in an astonishing new cooperation while the war went on in Bosnia.

As modern man makes his life forever more complicated, he builds up his fool's paradise more and more dominated by the falsity of modern science, politics, and technology.

The Empty-Headed Savage

Man is human, which is the opposite of the science and technology he has developed too quickly in the 20th century, and reveres so ludicrously to the point of idolatry, as he prepares to enter the 21st century.

The result of this idolatry and the rise of the power of the computer and the Internet, instead of liberating man to a higher quality of life, may be pushing him right back to his former misery and enslaved state.

Modern man, the empty-headed savage, had every opportunity to choose a more intelligent style of life than he did. He had that power, where most animals do not, and he bungled tragically all his best chances for real human progress.

The scientific discovery that man uses only a very minuscule part of the full potential of his brain is very conveniently swept under the rug of his consciousness so that he can continue his modern path to slavery and subservience to science and technology.

The likelihood that the human part of the brain that develops great abilities in science and technology is also minuscule, seems both logical and scientifically well-founded.

Modern man selects his false leaders and his false style of life, even though he does not have to. The result of this idolatry of plain and crude materialism is a great loss in the basic joys and energies of life, and the spread of the social malaise, violence, and depression that contaminate modern human life, even in the world's richer nations.

Ancient man may have been much wiser than modern man in selecting his basic joys and directions of energy in life because his scientific and technological ego remained much less developed and much more humble than modern man's.

The power to communicate is a simple power common to many living species. Unfortunately, man, the empty-headed savage, thinks that he has a unique ability to communicate that makes him the most intelligent and superior living species.

The power to communicate, just like any other power, is only as good as the results it is used for. Man has no monopoly on morality, since many animals seem to have developed a higher ethical code of conduct.

Human dictators, politicians, and exploiters of common evil all develop persuasive abilities to communicate. Human history and its tale of horror of most of man's past human leadership, raises much doubt and suspicion upon the true value of the ability to communicate.

Modern man, with his music, his television, and his computers hooked up to the Internet, has become a sometimes dangerous addict of false communication. Often, violent criminals have claimed that it was loud music and pictures that spurred them to atrocious evil.

Modern man's ability to communicate may not be half as good as he imagines, unless he can improve his character and willpower to use it more wisely. Once again, with the tiny part of his brain that he uses, modern man has developed the potential and extent of his mechanical powers of communication, far ahead of any pragmatic and constructive use for them.

The power of aggressive and loud music to incite hate, violence, and evil, have been observed, confirmed, and confessed to. Both Jesus Christ and the devil have been attested to being excellent communicators.

Homo sapiens, the empty-headed savage, takes great pride in his intelligence and reasoning power, even though he so seldom demonstrates them.

Man is such a great hypocrite, loving his vices so much more than his virtues. He uses his theater and communication industry to glamorize his vices more than his virtues. He uses contests, competitions, and his winning-at-all-cost philosophy to do the same. He will murder and rape to win some silly contest of human pride and prejudice.

Man deceives only himself and makes his own misery, but it is his leaders, experts, and scientists in modern life that have fabricated his fool's paradise. Nowhere more than at his most prestigious modern scientists' conferences does man better demonstrates his intellectual vacuity and great gullibility.

With Hitler, Stalin, the old British Empire, the new American Empire, and with the huge poor China thrown in, man has fully demonstrated his intellectual vacuity and empty-headedness in the 20th century and promises all too little for a better next century.

Science and technology made possible the huge increase in the immorality of modern warfare. Ancient man would send out his opposing army champions for honorable combat to death, with simple and clear victories assured. Modern man pushes his buttons of war, killing thousands of bystanders, damaging his environment for hundreds of years, and still not assuring himself of any clear-cut victory.

Modern man goes even further in his immorality and lunacy, with his rich industrialized nations competing and peddling their sophisticated and very expensive weapons of war to poorer countries who cannot afford them. The result has been thousands of wars in the 20th century, with deaths of innocents in the millions.

The great advances in modern man's science and technology may only flatter his already overblown ego, while reducing all other intelligences.

Wars are never justified and hardly ever result in the desired benefits for the empty-headed savage victor. Peddling weapons of war around the world and participating in one military adventure after another, changes the face of any democracy and turns it into just another imperialistic empire.

American military and economic imperialism after World War II required the price of abandoning the pursuit of democracy and heading the world toward globalization.

Globalism and the profit motive dominating the American economic system promoted corporate capitalism and political imperialism at the expense of political freedom, democracy, and the small individual capitalism of true free enterprise.

The great American Dream of democracy, economic and political freedom, and independence were sacrificed for the imperialism of international power and prestige.

Worst of all for the empty-headed human savage at the end of the 20th century, modern science and technology were being used steadily to further enslave man, rather than to liberate him toward true human progress so that he could open his mind and learn to use the greatest part of the human brain that has remained so dormant and destructive throughout human history.

About Fear

Man is born with his instincts of fear just like other animals. These fears form a good part of human intelligence. When a child matures, human society starts interfering with the natural intelligence of fears, often harassing and distorting them. The probable result of this is that many animals remain more intelligent than humans in living with and dealing with their fears.

Whether man is a superior animal or not, he is a supreme hypocrite and he is corrupt so he will often use the distortion of fear to impose his will upon others for good or evil purposes and with good or evil results.

Man struggles so much in using his fears more intelligently because of his bloated ego so often forced upon him by his society. Animal societies may thus often use the instinct of fears more intelligently than man in developing techniques of survival and enhancing the quality of life.

Corrupt human society will often invent nonexistent fears in order to better manipulate individuals and control their freedoms. It will then completely deny the existence and resounding intelligence of many fears that could be used to enhance the quality of human life.

The folly of human society often forces man to lose much of the common sense and intelligence of his most natural instincts of fear. It is indeed ironic that Homo sapiens, the so-called wise animal, is so misled by his society in the intelligent use of his instincts, his senses, and his fears. It is a surrender of a superior and natural intelligence that could form unique individuals for the artificial intelligence that forms the mediocrity of conformity in human society.

Human society actually tries to regulate fear and to ruin its natural intelligence with the artificial and contrived judgments of societal corruption and falsity. When the great industrial revolution promised all men, no matter how poor and humble, some great benefits and a huge step forward in human progress, there was indeed plenty of skepticism and fear among the poor and downtrodden that the promise would never be fulfilled. Corrupt human society keeps using various fears and promises to keep the lid on human progress and to keep the special privileges flowing to the ruling class and the elite.

Fear is used by all governments, religions, and dictators of all kinds to keep their constituents servile and submissive. Man's artificial and societally contrived fear can lead even the most reasonable man to hysterics and dementia. False societal priorities create the fears that are not intelligent ones and too much fear of fears that lead all men astray, often toward great unhappiness and violence. Poor man becomes completely unreasonable and neurotic.

Ironically, a brave and courageous man cannot exist without fears because if he truly has no fear of anything he can be neither brave nor courageous. Heroes are so often portrayed by society as men or women without fear. No wonder that heroes who claim they are heroes are not, and those that society claims as heroes are hardly ever either. The politician and the mass media have a great stake in creating false heroes because they are both professional exploiters of human fears. The sensationalism that drives the modern mass media depends upon the hysterics of human fears. The politician uses character assassination of his opponents as an exploitation of fear.

Human leadership uses fear as its most prevailing weapon in suppressing, exploiting, and ruling all men. Humans are forced out of touch with their more intelligent fears and enslaved with the contrived fears formulated by the corruption of society. The leader becomes an expert at exploiting a thousand fears and will-fully mismanaging and manipulating those fears.

Man can live blindly, driven by imagined hate determined by false fear. The United States of America, the supposed bastion of democracy and tolerance, lived for fifty years in perpetual and hysterical fear of the Soviet Union. It plotted with, cooperated with, and even installed dictators with other vicious tyrannies, all because of its paranoiac fear of the Soviet Union; and all at great expense to its dedication to democracy.

Modern industrial man, and his deranged tyrants of materialism have made a mockery out of a vast array of intelligent human fears to replace them with a love of speed and consumption. Modern man loves speed, denies any justified fear of it, and loves it better than other qualities. Modern man, aided by science and technology, prefers speed with greed and quantity over character and quality. The result is that modern humans tend to overeat, overdrink, and then go out to speed in their merry automobiles, killing more humans than in all the wars in history.

Intelligent fear can lead to wisdom, caution, doubt, common sense, foresight, and other considerations far greater than an individual's ego or a tyrant's mad ambition and lust for power.

Nearly all major religions have used fanatic fear to lead their followers to commit horror and violence.

A dictator in China orders the massacre of thousands of his own people who were demonstrating peacefully for democracy.

Afterward, he confesses outright that he was afraid his own people were going to hurt him, so it was better to kill them than to lose his power by giving the people too much freedom. It is strange to think that a strong man kills because he is afraid and he is a coward. It is also strange that so many democracies support strong men in dictatorships around the world.

If man had character and was reasonable and honest, he would use all his fears constructively to build a peaceful and harmonious society. Instead, he prefers his vices and uses all his fears, real or contrived, to create his theaters of nonsense in his society or in his arts and entertainment medias. The modern mass media, with all its high technology, facilitates the multiplication and spread of all of man's vices and folly instead of trying to do the opposite.

It is unfortunate that so many achievers were driven to success by fear rather than real quality. A famous comedian was driven to success by a threatening and abusive father. A great athlete did not even like the sport in which he excelled because he had been forced into it, cruelly, as soon as he had outgrown his diapers. Not only can character and quality be killed by fear, but also a philosophy of winning at all costs can be born and rooted in fear.

Human society is ruled more by competition and the corruption and distortion of fear and violence than it is ruled by democracy. Some men fear democracy as much as they pretend to love it. As long as human leadership depends on fear to rule, it will remain as destructive as in the past.

Competition and Winning at All Costs

When man came to earth he had to face the problem of competition just like the other animals and forms of life. As soon as man started to feel more intelligent than the other forms of life, he had to deal with all the problems of competition and try to rise above its often devastating destructive side. It is undoubtedly a more intelligent man who first observed that the man who always won, often lost more than he actually gained, and that the man who often lost, gained more than he lost. Even the most backward caveman could understand and rebel against the senseless destructiveness of all-out competition.

Children are often more perceptive than adults when they detect the absurdity and stupidity existing in all-out competition. They often display hilarious disgust with the competitive games that adults force them to play, and sometimes they show an amazing courage in refusing to participate.

Unfortunately, human society has not progressed very much in dealing with all the problems of competition. A certain amount of

competition among humans may be necessary and fairly constructive, but too much competition is contrived by the corrupt, senseless, false priorities of society. Idolatry of competition, just for competition's sake, leads too often to destructive jealousy and violence.

Often, an intelligent man will notice that when he runs ahead
of anybody else in competition, he will surely win a medal, but if
he falls too suddenly, he will surely be stepped on by more than
one. He will soon realize that going slower than the competition
may not be only more intelligent but much safer.

A very cultivated man finds out early that the greatest
human creators and achievers in human history managed to iso-
late themselves and they were often ridiculed as societal out-
siders. Quality and excellence for the truly great achievers were
products of within and not from any competition with any others. Mindless competition produced only more inferiority and
never any true superiority.

The gods of competition flatter mainly all the devils in
human vices that have ruled for so long in human society. All-
out competition and winning at all costs mainly feeds the
overblown egos, waste, and irresponsibility of special privileges.
Competition rarely provides all it promises, nor is it practiced
very often by its strongest advocates. Competition is often an
enemy to freedom and democracy and an invitation to tyranny
and corruption.

In human economics, competition is not always allied to
quality and free enterprise. In politics, competition usually guar-
anties the rule of incompetents, giving all the wrong people too
much power and then proving that power corrupts one and all.
The simple truth that the enlarged ego of man hates to admit, is
that the vast majority of normal men have rather similar abilities,
and many men with rather inferior abilities often outperform
other men with greater abilities.

Winning at all costs is no less than competition gone completely berserk. It is competition bound to become short on quality and creativity. Far too many men use competition for mere exhibitionism and boosting of their egos, instead of increasing their abilities and performances.

Far too many modern sports are cheap exhibitionism, more than they are any great displays of physical skill. Ugly competition often ruins the wholesome purpose of the sport. Instead of building character, it corrupts and breeds violence.

As much as some of the more intelligent children protest being pushed by their parents into unwanted competition, most eventually have to capitulate. Crime, violence, and many other ills in human society are much more associated with society's immature attitude toward competition than most modern social scientists would ever admit. Ironically, the competition of necessity and survival among animals seems often more reasonable than many of the competitions organized by humans for humans.

In studying the derelicts and dropouts of human society, it is always quite surprising to find so many great achievers and competitors among them who had suddenly become nauseated with the fierceness of competition and refused to continue. It is not surprising that those who make the rules for others to compete, as well as the elite, hardly ever have to compete too fiercely themselves.

History shows how often those who make the rules of competition in society cheat, steal, or murder in all-out efforts to eliminate their own competition. Children learn about the hypocrisy of competition, not only in their families, but in their schools. They find out very early in their lives that too many winners of competitions are very flawed and suspect in character. Only a very stupid man will ever claim that he is the absolute best on earth in some endeavor in which he excels.

Because the rules and judgments in human contests and competitions are so often hypocritical and subjective, the winners are bound to be equally as feeble. It has been found too often that the winners in competitions seldom live up to either their own expectations or those of society in the long run. It is obvious that an obsessive desire to win at any cost flaws both performance and achievement.

Humans are quite famous for displaying the most terrible sportsmanship in societies that preach the winning at all costs philosophy. This can lead directly to cheating, tragedy, disgrace, and even murder; and there should be no surprise in the cruelty, bad character, corruption, and destruction in such a society.

Human society insists upon making false idols and heroes out of ugly winners of competitions. These poor winners become the monsters who run rampant throughout society, destroying all the more noble values of man.

Only a very stupid man will ever profess any absolute certainty in pronouncing judgment upon the intelligence of other men, but here again modern society encourages just that. Surveys have been made upon the competitive scores in scholastic examinations given in so many universities. Educators were humiliated in finding out how poor a criterion in intelligence scores in scholastic tests really were when they tracked the future of their students years after graduation.

It was found that those scoring the highest in academic tests were rarely the most brilliant in their future lives. The obvious conclusion is that human competition rarely produces any formidable benefits, reminding all men that winner take all is totally destructive.

Contests, competitions, and scholastic achievements have to be rewarded reasonably if they ever want to aspire to the general good of society. If winners are rewarded too extravagantly they are bound to become self-destructive. Already, most second and third place contestants usually do get rewarded, but rewards should go down the line much further because no one contestant should be rewarded more that ten times any other contestant.

There are far too many fallacies produced by competitions that they should not be relied on so heavily to decide the social, economic, and political priorities of society. There is far too much evidence that unlimited competition becomes suicidal. Modern man fabricates his fool's paradise based on his idolatry of competition, leading to unlimited consumption and self-destruction, killing all other living species that may hinder his lust and his greed. Fierce competition kills humanism and can return man back to barbarism and cruel savagery.

There is little doubt that competition, speeded up by science and technology, is potentially threatening to the very survival of man and his planet. Berserk competition within any one entity nearly always kills the whole, once it becomes too fierce and loses all harmony and purpose.

Man is full of contradictions, and according to Oscar Wilde, there are two human tragedies; one is getting what one wants, and the other is not getting it. So it is that a winner can become a loser and the loser can become the real winner.

About Violence

Every human learns at an early age what violence is— especially human violence. Most humans are deeply affected and disillusioned by society's corruption by tolerating and even condoning human violence.

The idolatry of competition and winning at all costs, the speed and greed of a nation's corrupted false economic priorities and work ethic, contribute handily to the widespread acceptance and encouragement of human violence.

The human individual becomes a witness, sometimes a participant, and often a victim of violence, and his reactions can be highly unpredictable, according to his own demons and the false dictates of his society.

Individual and communal hypocrisy seem nearly always evident in all matter dealing with human violence. Modern sports, among many other human activities, form just one of the corrupted arenas promoting human violence.

The pathology of human leadership shows that far too many of the most powerful leaders in history have been very inferior men in their thirst for power, their love of competition, and the corrupted use of violence in pursuing their fame and glory. Most leaders have been great hypocrites in demanding sacrifices and a slave work ethic from others, while basking themselves in leisure, luxury, and glory.

Scientists suspect that some humans are born with an errant gene that makes them prone to unreasonable anger and violence. Some babies can throw fits of violence at their mother's breast, but they usually have better reasons than the deranged leaders of the world who have been preaching and practicing human violence throughout history.

Surely the false social, economic, and political priorities of modern scientific man in the 20th century have increased his hypocritical tolerance, promotion, and secret admiration of human violence.

Modern man's violence helped his lightning fast advances in science and technology, leading to his ostentation, consumption, speed, greed, and waste. Modern man's new style of life was full of self-indulgence, steeped in constant change or the fear of it, in the midst of his mindless competition, aggression, and violence.

Modern capitalistic economic systems that brag about their political democracy, their free enterprise, their free markets, their fair competition, and an honorable work ethic with an equitable distribution of wealth, never stop lying.

These lies too often lead to social strife, riots, and violence. Capitalism is an empty word that has ruled the world ever since the Roman Empire days and before. It forms one of the greatest parts in the tragedy of human history, and all the mostly failed efforts to reform it.

Human progress has a life of its own in spite of the greedy and the powerful, while life in the fast lane of modern industrial society confesses to its great vacuity, anxiety, and hopelessness. The false economic, social, and political priorities promote human exploitation and corruption, along with the fear of poverty and violence.

Nationalism, religion, and the profit motive become the main accomplices in a new modern tyranny of consumption, greed, fear, and violence.

A great new social malaise spreads throughout the world as modern man's speed and greed rise to forever greater levels for potential self-destruction.

The embarrassment of modern man's rising tide of senseless crime, violence, and wars precludes all claims of progress and achievement. The social scientists, the politicians, the religious leaders, and the ever present mass media meet on a regular basis to discuss the phenomenon in search of solutions.

The solutions always seem as clear as the total lack of political will and morality of modern man in implementing them. Crime and violence are the direct result of modern man's social, economic, and political ills.

Several American presidents, including Ronald Reagan and George Bush, cowardly refused all serious efforts at controlling the widespread availability of murderous assault weapons to the general public. The pathology and cowardice of human leadership cannot be ignored, nor can any valid excuses be invented.

The National Rifle Association, dishonest politicians, and the thirst for power are among some of the reasons. The almighty profit motive, competition, and winning at all costs are other reasons. The speed and greed and the all around corruption of modern society are the main reasons that a simple thing like keeping murderous weapons out of reach of the general public becomes practically impossible.

Violence does not have to be a completely irrational act of the last resort when a man abandons all restraint, intelligence, and moral reason. Violence can be premeditated and more cowardly. Both presidents Ronald Reagan and George Bush were caught in scandals of international armament dealing, spreading violence and terrorism around the world.

These respected patricians of their society had evidently

learned the use and love of violence at the hands of their educators in their ambitious pursuit of power, fame, and glory.

The problems with modern man's daily acceptance of violence seems to become insurmountable in view of the horrendously bad example of most of his leadership. It appears to be a miracle that man ever reaches his adulthood without becoming himself a witness, addict, or victim of crime or violence.

Small wonder that the military in peacetime are honored and coddled at great expense to human progress and society, rather than being disbanded as the great blight that it is.

Violence is man's ultimate pitfall, the proof that he has not progressed much further than any other animal. How long will it take for man to overcome this handicap is anybody's guess, but until then man has very little claim to any meaningful progress.

About Speed

M an has had a long, childish love affair with speed, but it is only modern man, thanks to his science and technology, who wallows in it and has become addicted to it.

Speed may be the greatest defect in modern man's intellect. Learn faster, think faster, move faster, build faster, and destroy faster. Modern society wants man to run, compete, and consume faster and faster. The speed and greed of modern man's sciences and technologies have no end in sight, making modern man's whole lifestyle become absurd and senseless.

Fast cars, airplanes, and food lead to fast thinking and too many errors. The result is total boredom and mediocrity. Excessive speed leads to chaos and confusion—then to destruction.

Common sense teaches man that the intelligence of excessive speed is very limited. Modern man's machines are very fast and they make him run, consume, and destroy much faster than is good for his health.

Curiously, it may be a defect in the pure scientific brain that fails to notice that speed in itself offers no proof of greater human intelligence. Quite the contrary, there is much evidence that speed may hinder both intelligence and common sense.

The moronic philosophy of modern man's speed causes countless human casualties. The faster man runs, the more he loses his freedom along with the pleasure of smelling the flowers of his earth.

The faster man runs, the easier it is for him to be controlled and enslaved by his human exploiters. Intelligence leads to wisdom, only with time and not with speed. Wisdom can withstand all the temptations of speed.

Modern scientific man, as well as most other men, use only a tiny fraction of their brains. The addiction to speed tempts all men to act more hastily than to think clearly and intelligently.

Most men hate the truth and are the last to recognize it. Modern man thinks that the faster he can learn something and use it to change some of the conditions in his life, the more he is displaying his higher intelligence and the more he will improve. Tragically, as history fully demonstrates, this thinking is more a dream than reality. Millions and millions of humans have been killed or maimed by modern man's speed and greed.

Hitler and many other mad totalitarian dictators and human exploiters, worked closely with the scientific community to dominate and enslave their people. It is clear that too many hasty social and economic changes nearly always leave a long trail of human victims.

The faster that modern man runs and travels, the less he sees clearly and thinks intelligently. The speed of social and economic changes works to favor human exploiters and dictators.

Modern man completely misjudges true human intelligence in his admiration of speed and competition and his addiction to consumption and technology. He relegates those who think more slowly and intelligently to become social outcasts, and sometimes declares them misfits.

Modern man's intelligence is so related to the speed, memory, and overload in his sciences and technologies that he has completely forgotten the whole purpose of intelligence.

The logical main purpose of all human intelligence would seem to have to be directly involved with providing man with a much higher quality to his life.

Instead, modern man gives away this most important part of his intelligence to the mercy of his speed, machines, and their artificial intelligence. He refuses to take the time to think.

Speed is modern man's aphrodisiac that dulls his brain. He uses it in everything he does, picking most of his fruit before it is ripe enough, and ruining much of what his earth provides that is best for him.

The great scientist Albert Einstein, late in his life, seemed to often warn modern scientific man of the great dangers of moving ahead too quickly in new scientific discoveries and technologies. A more mature Einstein became perturbed at the probability of frequent scientific error, its certainty, and of course the increasing potentially disastrous result of it.

As a man of tremendous intelligence, Einstein despaired later in his life that modern man's intellectual development was not keeping pace with his too rapid advances in science and technology.

Einstein and a few other brilliant scientists started to regret their own discoveries and the speed in their revelations to the rest of the world.

Modern man does not seem to understand that bowing down too much to the gods of speed, competition, and the artificial intelligence of his computer machines, make him lose too much of his individual freedom and his versatility of mind and body.

The automobile, the airplane, and the computer are probably modern man's most destructive speed machines. The automobile kills millions of people, the airplane had been used to bomb millions, and the computer stores release too much information for the sanity and good health of most men.

The computer pushes human life beyond the natural course

of wisdom. Nothing would seem more ridiculous concerning speed and time than the commentary of the highly skilled scientists who were reviewing the achievements of the American Voyager II spacecraft as it moved relatively close to Triton, a moon of Neptune. These highly skilled scientists' only intelligible comment was a nonsensical, "Wow!" It had taken years for the Voyager to reach the general area of Neptune, and it was expected to take another 40 years for it to reach any other area close enough to be regarded as a practical objective.

Nothing would seem to be lacking more in common sense and human intelligence, let alone human compassion, in this wasteful endeavor at a time when millions of human beings around the world were starving to death. It was a spectacular display of man's inhumanity to man, in broadcasting such an extravagant welfare program for the already rich scientists of the world, while not providing for all the poor, starving people of the world.

The relativity between science, technology, speed, time, the human ego, consumption, greed, and cost was completely lost upon the one-track mind of the rich, government-supported scientific community. There was a total lack of understanding between science, the human ego and arrogance, and a genuine pursuit of human progress. Spectacular pursuits of science and the development of mass destructive weapons can be counterproductive to progress.

The man who runs too fast and wins a great race, and the scientist and the mechanic who design and build great engines, leap in joy and pride in themselves. Arrogance and the human ego arrive on the scene of these everyday human achievements, soon ruining all possible constructive effects.

It is speed and greedy thinking that are the main diseases of modern man and hold him back from ever achieving real human progress.

Terrorism

The modern empty-headed savage moves quickly between his competition, violence, and speed to eventually graduate to terrorism. Modern man's terrorism is often even more vicious than his more formally declared wars. In declared wars, man has certain rules of human decency based on the Geneva Convention or the threat of Vienna-type war criminal trials. Terrorism does not recognize any bounds of human decency and its guerrilla tactics can be used by any aggressive individual, nation, political group, criminal band, or religion.

Terrorism kills, destroys, and maims just like full scale wars, but with better chances that the cowardly perpetuators can escape unpunished. Superpowers engage in terrorism just like everybody else, but they rarely admit it. Economic sanctions are a form of terrorism, particularly cowardly, that starve and kill innocent people for some perceived misdeeds of their leaders. Superpowers engage in terrorism by covert military actions, armament dealing, secret alliances, and brutal economic blackmail, all to expand or solidify their spheres of influence.

The United Nations has found itself too often the perfect foil, behind which too many nations can hide their terrorism. Nearly all great colonial powers and military empires have engaged in more than their fair share of terrorism. The constant threat of the United States dropping atomic bombs on any nation which displeased it was a thinly disguised act of terrorism. The long protracted Cold War between the American and Soviet military empires was a breeding ground for terrorism. The toll in innocent victims in neutral nations was horrendous and never inscribed in history books.

It was strange for the American voters to find out for sure, during the Ronald Reagan and George Bush administrations, that their nation dealt in international terrorism. American presidents sold arms illegally and set up international terrorism covertly. Saddam Hussein, the most famous of all international terrorists, had been helped by the American presidents in Iraq's long protracted war against a more feared Iran. But then, Saddam Hussein turned against his master, the American president, and tried to bite the hand that had fed him.

The result of that bit of misguided American international terrorism turned out to cost the American taxpayers countless billions of dollars in the Persian Gulf War and its aftermath. Millions of completely innocent people were affected and died as a result of the American presidents' folly. The word terrorism is nearly always associated with the word coward. France decided it did not like an anti-nuclear bomb organization called Greenpeace, so its agents blew up one of their boats in its harbor.

Terrorism becomes more real and frightening when it starts to hit closer and closer to home. All American citizens were shocked with the reality of the Twins Tower bombing in the thick of New York City. Only a couple of years later they witnessed the bombing of a federal building in Oklahoma City, with horrendous casualties of completely innocent men, women, and children. Americans were horrified to find out that terrorism could also be domestic rather than international.

Throughout history, religion has always had a strong showing in terrorism. Many of the worst recorded acts of genocide in human history were instigated by the fanatic terrorism of religion.

The abortion clinic bombings in the United States and the murder of several people in attendance at these clinics were new forms of terrorism by crackpot religious fanatics. The mass suicides arranged by the leaders of several religious cults worldwide were the works of terrorism of the control artists and human exploiters under the umbrella of religion. Religion was an easy place to hide behind for dedicated self-glorifiers and power seekers with fanatic views.

Guerrilla warfare and terrorism defeated and humiliated the United States in Vietnam. A huge expensive modern military machine fell apart in the face of well-directed terrorism in the capable hands of a valiant enemy. The North Vietnamese were truly masters of psychological warfare, while the Americans were soft and lost all their military discipline and self-esteem. Vietnam was truly one of the most amazing defeats of a major military power by a second rate power in the history of man.

Terrorism thrives in great revolutions where a nation's long established power structure collapses. The Reign of Terror in the French Revolution was a period in the middle of the revolution, where terror and mass murder completely ruled a whole nation therefore deemed to be civilized. Terrorism nearly always emanates from various political institutions, social or religions institutions, secret associations, or not-so-secret organizations.

The cowardly terrorist nearly never acts without some outside organized encouragement. In the United States, the groups that hypocritically encourage crime and terrorism have been quite easily identified, but the political establishment has also been implicated in the perfidy of their continuous success.

Power corrupts one and all, especially in the cowardly use of terrorism. Even the Holy Catholic Popes engaged in disgraceful terrorism at the time of the Great Inquisition. History proves that American presidents have not shied away from soiling their honor in cowardly terrorism on both the domestic and international front. Ronald Reagan and George Bush were both involved in establishing the terrorist power of Saddam Hussein of Iraq and then bowing to the special interests of the crude American Rifle Association. The American presidents' support of terrorism surely killed thousands of innocent people at home and abroad.

Great economic disparity and injustice in the general population of any republic or democracy leads directly to terrorism. In recent modern American history, the disastrous Los Angeles riots and the Oklahoma City Federal Building bombing were caused by the economic outcasts of the nation. Both Reagan and Bush were leaders in the economic terrorism against the American middle class and the working man, in full complicity with their own special privileges and payoffs from the corporate world.

Domestic terrorism exists in the escalating crime rate of the nation, caused by poverty and unemployment that lead directly to drug abuse, alcohol, and violence. As the wealth gap increases in an economic system obsessed with the profit motive and the special interests of the large insensitive commercial corporations, the likelihood and the certainty of domestic terrorism increases. Much of the violence fermented in religious cults are related to economic dropouts. There is a certain amount of terrorism for the vast majority of the American people who are fed up with the nation's bankrupt two major political party system.

The insensitive George Bush claimed that the United States of America needed to become a kinder, gentler nation. As he was engaging in foreign terrorism, he was afraid of terrorism that could explode in his own nation. Terrorism is a cowardly act, regardless of whether it is internal or external, or committed by the political establishment or the outsider. George Bush and the

Catholic popes during the Great Inquisition, were part of the establishment, living opulent lives far above most of their constituents, and their terrorism was aimed at maintaining their love of power. Human leaders have always had the knack of letting others do their dirty work.

Modern day terrorism comes from the naive admiration of man for competition, power, aggression, and violence—both physical and intellectual. The gentle philosopher has been replaced in modern society by the aggressive technocrat, bureaucrat, merchant, or politician driven by the love of power and the profit motive. Globalization helps modern day terrorism tremendously by keeping oppressive dictatorships in power much longer than needed for human progress.

Another very telling form of terrorism has risen with a very gullible modern man's idolatry of science and technology. Modern man's computer and information superhighways may possibly be used one day to spread uncontrolled terrorism around the world.

Misleading
the World

History is so absurd because it hardly ever tells the truth. Struggles for human rights and democracy occur throughout the ages, while revolutions have an ominous habit of turning in full circle, but not far enough from the starting point. The modern history of man is not very long and it is mostly all about the failure of man in forming his nations and empires.

The tale of barely a dozen great empires sums up most of man's known history. Who would have thought that an upstart breakaway colony of the former British Empire would so quickly become the next superpower? The United States thus takes its place among a whole list of great nations and empires, while the former Soviet Empire falls apart. Power corrupts one and all and the same capitalistic economic system that has ruled the world since the Roman Empire days easily shucks off most of the pitiful efforts to reform its injustice.

History changes continuously according to the reigning superpower of the moment. The greatest war in human history, World War II, won by the Soviet Union and the former British Empire with the support of the United States, suddenly becomes a strictly great American victory. The right of a superpower to suddenly change history is as old as history itself. Small wonder that the greatest empire in human history, the Ottoman Empire, can fade so quickly into memory.

Empires and superpowers show a startlingly similar course of successes and failures, nearly always to unpredictable and sometimes sudden decline. Throughout the whole farce of history, the struggle for human rights and dignity remains rather unchanged.

Nationalism, militarism, and empiricism were the main enemies of democracy and the people. This was declared by the main founders of the United States of America as they swore to never be lured into their trap. The budding new nation in North America remained safe from these nefarious ambitions for only a few short years.

Success in competition, even among nations, nearly always leads to megalomania and self-destruction that hinders democracy and self-improvement. It is the rarest of all men and all nations who can handle success with reason and dignity. Human leadership in history proves only one thing and that is how poor it has been. The average ant colony lives more harmoniously than most of the human race has ever lived.

The vast majority of all human leaders are much more followers than they are ever leaders. That is one reason human history is so absurd. The mother of the Great Napoleon observed that, unfortunately, he was the least endowed of her many children. The Great Napoleon made a lot of noise and gathered a lot of fame in his lifetime, but for the vast majority of men he was a disaster, killing millions of them.

History shows how slow human progress and achievement have been. It is too often the human leaders who are the monsters who slow down and deny human progress. It is too often the leaders of the nations who order genocide and mass deportation, establishing and supporting other leaders in the world who do the same.

The human race seems to have produced only a handful of real leaders whose ideas lived longer than they did. The message seems to be that good ideas are much more important than the identity of any leader.

When the United States entered World War II, its leadership never realized that it would be losing most of its national independence and its military security by being on the winning side. The American leadership fell prey to the lure of power, greed, and ambition just like the leadership of other great military powers had done after the glory of a great military victory.

Only a few years after World War II, the Americans were changing history, declaring themselves the sole and primary victors of the war. The main participants in that war, namely the Soviet Union and Great Britain, were all but forgotten as the real heroes of the war. The leadership of the Soviet Union and the United States immediately started another devastating war, the Cold War, and democracy was all but forgotten for fifty years.

History lies. Wars are nearly always lost by both sides, no matter how much the winner beats his chest in proclaiming victory. History lies. Economics has more to do with starting wars than nearly any other factor. Only a few years after World War II, the United States started to decline as a great nation and an economic powerhouse.

In a short fifty years, the American family was broken up economically, with both parents struggling in the workplace to feed their children. The United States had become the prime policeman of the world and had lost its sovereignty to the United Nations. Its leadership had engaged in terrorism around the world and became the main pusher of a new world order, based on economic development and greed, called globalization.

Human ideas often become runaway ideas that kill, starve, and maim millions and millions of people.

The individual human rights ideas in history have been much stronger than all the dictators and other human exploiters trying to kill them. Jesus and Buddha may be the only true leaders in the short history of man. Lasting ideas are stronger than any human individual and sometimes produce unexpected surprises.

None of the elite intelligentsia predicted the sudden demise of the Soviet Empire, nor the decline of the American Empire, nor the spectacular rise of China. Ronald Reagan and George Bush turned out to be the worst presidents of the United States. They accomplished the exact opposite of what they claimed. Reagan escalated the American government's deficit to unprecedented levels, and Bush led the nation into its first completely immoral war in the Persian Gulf, killing thousands of innocent foreigners, and losing the nation's military honor, security, and independence.

Too often, mad and devious humans in their pursuit of power follow the most corrupt ideas. Often they are too cowardly to openly admit the ideas they are pursuing. Hitler, Mussolini, Stalin, and many more so-called leaders in human history were such men. They advocated dictatorship, militarism, and genocide, and they helped ruin most of the noble ideas in humanity.

Often, good ideas are so poorly thought out by the corrupt human elite that they lead to exact opposite directions than originally intended. Many of man's incomplete social, political, and economic ideas do more to promote and coddle human vices than they ever reward human virtues. Capitalism, communism, socialism, democracy, religion, nationalism, racism, globalism, and many other ideas represent the multitude of human failures that hinder man's progress.

Strong men with bad ideas become weak, while weak men with good ideas become strong, but strong men with good ideas are extremely rare.

History shows how human society is so usually corrupt and rewards human vice and hypocrisy more than virtue. Small wonder that the false heroes rule most often and that capitalism has been so impossible to reform. History also shows the false heroes forever misleading the entire human race, always proclaiming they are the greatest, and thinking they are worth a million other men. History also shows that as soon as man departs from his good and noble ideas, he sinks into the clutches of his false gods and heroes. As soon as capitalism and democracy does not serve the best interests of the greatest possible majority of the people, it falls into the hands of greedy power hungry individual or corporate human exploiters.

History continually lies and shows only how long and how far the human race has been mislead. True leaders have been so rare that no one man or one nation can stand up completely proud and tall in any record of true and inspiring leadership.

Man, the incredible coward, competitor, and power seeker, always hides behind his hypocrisy. Exclusive families, clubs, institutions, and corporations are perfect places for cowardly and devious men to hide.

The modern politician is the great hypocrite and power broker who enters these exclusive clubs in his unsatiable thirst for power, glory, and fame.

Modern man and his over-educated fool's paradise of a society is full of these specialized clubs, all competing jealously for outlandish power and special privileges, denying democracy and human progress.

History shows that democracy has never existed, and that man hates his freedom and prefers his enslavement. Capitalism is man's best guaranty of his continued enslavement, and the more unbridled capitalism becomes, the better it can serve the purpose of human exploitation and dictatorship.

Socialism, of course, is a persistent enemy of unbridled capitalism, but it is mostly a failure as a desperate cry for some human democracy and progress.

Communism was the greatest tragedy of the 20th century, because it was a mere ploy of a mad dictatorship that created a typical human hallucination that never really existed.

The American Empire and last remaining superpower is just another one in a long line of capitalist dictatorships in history that have misled man so far away from democracy.

The American presidents have been mostly inept and inferior men, totally compromised and lacking in human leadership. The dying American devotion to democracy faces formidable opponents in the dictatorships of China and other populous nations, mastering unbridled capitalism.

As everywhere else in history, modern man hallucinates and continues to fabricate his own misery. He has much to be ashamed of in his 20th century with the disaster of his communism and fascism, so resembling each other, and his capitalism so unrepenting for having caused such disasters.

Hallucinating

Modern man hallucinates more than any of his predecessors, especially among his elite and his intelligentsia. One of the reasons for this has been his rapid advances in science and technology and the awful new entity known as the modern mass media.

The Cold War was probably man's longest and most senseless exercise in statesmanship, intellectual foresight, and futility. It was a period of building up an American and a Chinese empire and destroying the Soviet Empire. It was a period of regressing democratic aspirations around the world in favor of economic obsession with globalization.

The great advances in modern science and technology, having occurred much too rapidly for man's slow wit and intellect, made him more stupid rather than more intelligent. It is admittedly during this period that the great American dream of political, economic, and social progress faded to the disappearing point.

One of the many products of modern science and technology, the mass media, became the most abusive to human progress by its sensationalism that elevated its entertainment of human vices far above virtue, human progress, and social responsibility. The mass media simply became another tool of human enslavement and hallucination, rather than any strong progressive voice for man's enlightenment.

History lies about the rise in the mass media's power to negatively influence and subjugate the whole human race by its representation and interpretation of information and its awesome ability to create false idols and heroes. In just one instance it can completely destroy the democratic process of any nation by simply dictating whom it chooses to glorify.

The mass media, aided by science and technology, becomes the perfect foil and medium of modern man's hallucinations. The glorious vain absolutely love it, and so would have the Great Napoleon. President Richard Nixon loved it when it was on his side and hated it when it scoured him, but regardless, he still used his secret tapes to leave behind forever a lasting monument to his intellectual and moral corruption.

The list of hallucinations created by the modern mass media is as long as it is frightening. The power to constantly create false heroes and celebrities increases dependence upon science and technology. Pathetic men like Henry Kissinger, Ronald Reagan, and George Bush were coddled by the mass media to wreak havoc upon the United States.

The constant run of dunces into the White House can be directly attributed to the hallucinations of the mass media. The morally corrupt can be completely whitewashed by a hallucinating mass media. Lee Atwater, the Republican political party's tactician who engineered George Bush's presidential election, died in March 1991 from a brain tumor at only 40 years old. Before dying he apologized profusely for his despicable character assassination of the Democratic candidate Governor Dukakis.

The American mass media not only did not apologize for its part in false character assassination, but it kept on eulogizing Lee Atwater in his full corruption, even after his death. Atwater was at least honest in his efforts to lie, deceive, and distort public information to serve the corrupted political ambitions of his masters, but the nation's mass media remained completely shameless.

The mass media hallucinates as it becomes more powerful and sometimes it even pretends to search its soul. It destroys most of the noble ideas of man, more than it ever builds them up, by its great hypocrisy and insincerity in underexposing the nobility of man and overexposing man's corruption and debauchery.

As man prepares to enter the 21st century, history shows that he has hallucinated socially and economically for most of the past century. He has gone full cycle in the total corruption of capitalism. His economic disarray and social injustice are just as bad at the end of the century as they were at the beginning.

Science and technology, along with corporate capitalism, seem to have taught man absolutely nothing of real practical use during the whole century, so that he would have better guidelines in reaching out for human progress.

The modern computer, with the Internet and the Information Super Highway, only help man's totally inept intellect to become even more confused, and then to completely forget man's more noble ideas that took so many centuries to develop. Good and noble ideas grow forever slowly from the full context of the human intellect, while science and technology emanate from such an insignificant segment of the human brain.

There is nothing elevating on the part of modern human society in rewarding the arrogant mad dog human exploiters and specialists in self-glorification, while ignoring the real workers and producers in society. In all honesty, no one man is worth more than a hundred other men. Democratic ideas and principles are not mirages on computer screens. They are really quite simple deductions of the human intellect.

The mass media loves to make heroes out of the most outrageous egocentric and least deserving compositions of man in modern society; athletes, singers, entertainers, and politicians of too many stripes. The mass media is a salesman and it thrives on its cult of false heroes, helping destroy most of the best principles of democracy by paying too much attention to the least deserving members of society.

The modern day politician is probably one of the most dishonest compositions of man ever devised by his society. In the United States, a look at the steady stream of dunces arriving in and out of the White house proves the point.

The mass media and history lie. Modern man is not very intelligent. Chernobyl, the Three Mile Island nuclear accident in Pennsylvania, other disastrous industrial accidents, earthquakes, and natural disasters may have a much stronger impact on the human race than all his erratic and facetious politics.

History lies. There is far less difference between communism, socialism, and democracy than there is between a rich man and a poor man. The Chinese communists are proving that they can be super-millionaires also. Social and economic health are more important than politics and all the mad politicians.

The mass media, the politicians, science, technology, corporate enterprise, and globalization keep modern man far away from achieving any true acceptable human progress.

After all the politics and politicians in modern society, the weakest and most cowardly composition of man in society has to be the military man.

As long as standing armies are kept in peacetime by hundreds of powerful nations at exorbitant expense to them, there can never be meaningful peace and human progress in the world. As long as man has guns available to him and lusts for power, he will murder to gain that power. As long as man sells guns for profit, he can very well expect to be killed often by the gun he has sold.

As long as man cannot rise above his innumerable wars, human progress remains a mere hallucination. For the United States, the self-declared most moral nation in the world, its Persian Gulf War was an unprecedented descent into modern day barbarism. The United States fired the first shot, not honorably on the ground, but by bombing mostly innocent civilian targets of a very unlikely enemy. The United States had become the main designer of push button modern warfare, the most cowardly and barbaric ever devised by man.

In the greatest of all hallucinations, the American mass media started to push forward for serious presidential considerations the minor American army general in charge during the Persian Gulf strike by the name of Colin L. Powell. He was one of the push button generals with the stick and the charts, willing to bomb innocent people in order to remove their vicious tyrant, Saddam Hussein; but then letting the mad dog off scot-free, for so-called political reasons.

The American mass media had also made George Bush into a temporary hero in the Persian Gulf War, before turning viciously against him soon afterward.

Reality

Man's problem with accepting reality is probably his weakest characteristic, even though he likes to claim that he is the most intelligent living species on earth. The power of imagination, self-expression, and much of his perverted education, works constantly against a balanced and intelligent sense of reality.

History lies and is so tragic because man likes to live so far removed from reality. Small wonder that many animals seem more intelligent than man in adopting a sound and healthy life. The human elite, the power hungry, the intelligentsia, and the privileged seem to have the worst problems in living within reality.

Recognized human leadership is mostly myth and imagination because it usually acts contrary to what it preaches. In modern times, not a single truly recognized world leader or sanctified expert predicted the extent and sudden collapse of the Soviet Empire.

Man is truly a great hypocrite and nearly always refuses to admit to his own vices and absurdity. For instance, nearly all human economic systems preach about the importance of full employment and the welfare of the ordinary workingman and then blatantly connive against both.

Good ideas and human progress seem to have a life of their own. Man seems to recognize good ideas quite unanimously without argument, only to turn his back against them. He then becomes really ridiculous, marching off to war behind his mad popes, politicians, and generals, killing and destroying everything in his wake.

Man keeps acting against common sense and reality, while always promising to reform at some later date.

In a book of truths, power corrupts one and all, and the more absolute the power, the greater the chances of corruption.

There is no such thing as a just and honorable war, no matter what the corrupt politicians and the mass media pretend.

The golden rule is simply to treat others as one would wish to be treated. No man has either any right in a just democratic society to hoard and accumulate so much individual wealth that it gives him too much power so that he cannot possibly manage his wealth judiciously.

Neither greed nor violence are reasonable in human arguments and competitions. Extremism and fanaticism are also far removed from ordinary intelligence and common sense. In human politics, they lead directly to the devastating stupidity and waste in the eternal bickering between the liberal and the conservative. In religion, they lead directly to confrontation, violence, and genocide. In the military, they lead to widespread barbarity.

Kings, popes, and statesmen have been nothing more than failed politicians, basking in too much privilege and power, and still unable to compromise and live in peace and harmony.

The false reality is that man has all but abandoned his quest for democracy in individual independence and in political and religious freedom. The reality is that globalization and the United Nations are the new colonial powers that rule every aspect of modern man and dictate nearly all his freedoms. The United Nations and globalization have created a new wasteful, self-serving super elite with their corresponding expensive bureaucracies.

The reality is that the United States was the main bully in the United Nations, always trying to enforce most of its views and ambitions on the rest of the world.

Freedom and democracy and most of the promises made by the great industrial revolution of human progress for the ordinary working man, were sacrificed in favor of catering to globalization and the almighty dollar.

After the sudden collapse of the evil Soviet Empire, the U.S. demonstrated its own evil shoes. After all, its own mega corporate controlled economy was not too much more democratic than the central capitalism of the former Soviet Empire.

Instead of the former Soviet communist party economic heroes, the Americans created their own set of false economic corporate heroes and the new Russia adapted to the banditry of the American economic system which was neither very democratic nor anywhere close to true free enterprise.

Globalization killed true individual free enterprise and small capitalism as easily as American corporate capitalism had always tried to do. Globalization and the speed and greed of modern science and technology created a long list of false heroes in a corrupt elite, driven by false economic and social priorities.

Individual political, economic, and social freedom and independence had long been under attack in the United States by the robber barons of huge international corporations.

The assassination of the last progressive American president, John F. Kennedy, opened the doors to a new age of political cynicism that served the best interests of the new elite in large corporate towers, while abruptly halting human progress. Soon after would come the great debauchery of President Richard Nixon.

Another progressive American president, Dwight Eisenhower,

would write in his memoirs that Richard Nixon was the most dishonest man he had ever met in public life.

There is no greater fool than the over educated fool or the over exposed fool found so often in human history and in the modern mass media. The mass media is solidly under the control of mega-corporate commercialism. Richard Nixon found his ups and downs there, with the mass media never telling the truth about his severely disturbed personality.

The modern mass media rarely tells the truth. The impact on human society of Chernobyl and other disastrous modern industrial accidents is easily distorted and swept under the rug of human consciousness.

The truth that modern man's soul and most of his social, economic, and political progress have been sacrificed to the speed and greed of modern commerce, science, and technology, will hardly ever be revealed in a commercial mass media.

Modern man's pathetic dependence upon the innumerable and often poorly thought out and even dangerous products of modern industry grows forever greater. He creates his own doom and gloom in his pathetic need and dependence upon them. He then tends to abuse them so much that they do him more harm than any good.

Strong evidence exists that far too many products of modern industry, science, and technology are hastily devised and sold with only the almighty profit motive in mind and far too little thought for social need and responsibility.

In 1996, researchers at Fordham University declared that the American nation's social well-being index had been declining steadily for the past 25 years, with children and young people suffering the most.

More than one well recognized scientist has declared that there has not been a single essential scientific discovery made in the exorbitantly expensive manned American outer space program that could not have been made much more inexpensively in a laboratory.

It is modern man's unlimited selfish ego that drives him to ignore common sense and reality while he chases after artificial intelligence and virtual reality.

It is the great vanity of man that encourages him to spend more energy and resources in climbing higher mountains, or in conquering outer space, rather than tending to the quality of his every-day life. He is perfectly willing to allow his government to spend more on its welfare program for the already rich, like himself, rather than on any welfare program for the poor and disadvantaged.

A vain man wants to run before he can walk—he wants to conquer, kill, and dominate his environment before he masters himself and nurtures his fellow man.

An old Arab proverb proclaims that the name of fools is plastered on every wall. Human history, with the help of modern man's mass media, help spread this truth.

The best kept secret in history are the names of the real leaders in human society. As everyone knows, the real leaders of men are often the women behind them, as well as others who sacrifice and shun public exposure. The truly great leaders of men are bound to the secrecy of their great influence upon those who seek and lust for power. They are the people with good ideas, and exemplary conduct, living outside the public eye, who are often the mothers and fathers of their more famous offspring.

Small wonder that most leaders who think that they are such great leaders most often are not.

The modern day politician is so rarely a leader at all. He is much more a follower from one corruption to another, or from one folly to another. Witness Nixon and several other dunces who have lived in the White House.

The pathology of human leadership is as old as history itself. In man's most imperfect world, the power hungry and the corrupt rule more often than not.

It was easy for the U.S. to go to war in the Persian Gulf to protect foreign oil supplies that did not belong to them, when there was no moral leadership at home. It was also easy to spend three billion dollars arming the fanatic Mujahedeen Islamic fighters against the fast-fading Soviet Empire in Afghanistan and then walk away, not feeling the least bit guilty for the horrendous consequences that followed.

It was not so easy trying to use American influence and its military to stop the senseless genocide and mayhem in Bosnia when there was no oil supply or other monetary gain to protect.

The reality is that the American political leadership was not much different than the leadership of other previous great military empires. Unfortunately, the vast majority of ordinary Americans wanted something better than that. Much to their credit, most Americans wanted a more moral leadership.

The American Dream

The history of the United States of America is relatively very short—only a little over 200 years old—but it is also very long because it represents an age old struggle of man to find dignity and freedom in his life on earth. The American Dream was that there would finally be a nation of liberty, equality, and political freedom living in harmony and dignity. People from all over the world cast their eyes on the American Dream, and many rushed to the nation's new shores.

Unfortunately, at the beginning the new nation was nothing more than yet another British colony. The spirit of human freedom and a tax rebellion against the English monarchy, led to national independence in a War of Revolution. The new nation wrote a rather famous constitution which seemed to promise people around the world a real refuge from nationalism, militarism, and political oppression. Economics has nearly always much to do with political oppression or even genocide.

Even though the new nation was a republic rather than a democracy, it promised many new ventures in human progress. The great American Dream was being born that any man, regardless of his birth, could work hard and diligently in a new nation and expect to be justly rewarded. The great American Dream had its ups and downs in the new nation, and unfortunately peaked in the Golden Sixties during John F. Kennedy's presidency. Ever since then it has been declining rapidly as the United States insists upon misleading man into the 21st century, using the United Nations that it created to hide its imperialistic ambitions.

The American Revolution from Great Britain was supposed to create a truly independent nation, free of world imperialistic ambitions. The United States won a second war against England in 1812, fighting for its neutral rights against England's old imperialistic ambitions. The United States vowed to remain independent and to concentrate upon the welfare of its own people and all those who were flocking to its shores.

History shows how badly the United States has failed in its vow of independence and neutrality from old world imperialism. The United States had even failed to divorce itself completely from English influence and ambition. It rescued Great Britain twice in the two great wars of the 20th century, and walked into every international crisis fabricated by the fading British Empire. Dim-witted Ronald Reagan treated Margaret Thatcher as his very own queen, with the American people long used to paying for every whim of Great Britain.

Misguided American imperialism was lured into the disastrous Vietnam debacle, most probably to show off its military power and to show up the fading French colonial power. Both the French and the Americans were kicked out of Vietnam and Great Britain continued to brag that it never lost a war, especially when the Americans fought it for them. English national propaganda had truly succeeded in making American neutrality and independence dirty words in its former colony.

Great colonial powers do not give up very easily and the fading British empire had created explosive tinderboxes, not only in the Middle East, but everywhere else it had conquered. The

American problem was that their gullible presidents kept bailing out the fading British lion. The American people's problem was that they had become the scapegoat of stepping into the lion's shoes.

Economically, the United States had gone through extreme cycles of poverty and backwardness before reaching up to its wealthy superpower status. It obtained its worldly success through sheer diligence and hard work. The success of the American soldiers in World War I astounded both friends and foes. No soldier from any other nation worked so hard with so little and was so steadfast under fire. These were the American farm boys, called up to save Great Britain and Europe from the onslaught of Germany. But the world never learns and it wasn't over. Again, young Americans were called upon to sacrifice themselves for the mad Europeans in World War II.

Americans worked like fools for much less than their European brothers throughout most of modern history. The social benefits for the American working man always trailed the Europeans by scores of years. Only one American president, Franklin Delano Roosevelt tried his best to right the wrong. The Roosevelt influence carried the nation right to the Golden Sixties under John F. Kennedy, when the American workingman had finally arrived to hold his own. But that did not last long with the paranoiac politicians in Washington, D.C. and their self-destructive obsession with the Cold War and the Vietnam disaster.

History flies by and Sir Winston Churchill's dire prediction about the iron curtain proved terribly wrong, and so did the American conduct and strategy in the Cold War. The worst defeat for the American workingman was the fall of the Soviet Union. It gave all American industrial and commercial enterprise free reign to cultivate cheap foreign labor—even slave labor—to undercut their own people. The American president, Ronald Reagan, who had started it all, declared himself senile.

Without the image making and the hero fabrication by the mass media, Ronald Reagan could have never become president. As governor of California he had lashed out against all progressive communal programs, and he had failed dismally several times as a presidential candidate.

The ruthless and the power hungry never give up, and just like Richard Nixon before him, Ronald Reagan finally succeeded in his presidential ambitions.

Mr. Communicator right from the start, attacked the great American Dream by trying to eliminate many progressive programs, both in the United States and the United Nations. During Ronald Reagan's presidency, scores of Americans were imprisoned for asserting their freedom of speech. They were nearly all whistleblowers of some government corruption they had observed, and they paid the price for their unwanted revelations. The great communicator obviously wanted to be the only communicator.

During the 1992 presidential election campaign, the vast majority of Americans admitted freely that they would have preferred other choices than the ones forced upon them from behind the doors of the two major political parties' national conventions.

The mass media colluded with the power brokers and image makers by choosing the extent of the coverage they would accord any candidate.

The American Dream had always separated religion from government, but during Ronald Reagan's administration the fascism of religion was able to sneak aboard the political bandwagon with its now famous umbrella organization called the moral majority. Another safeguard of the American democracy was thus broken.

The religious right was led by power hungry television evangelists Jerry Falwell and Pat Robertson, a man who had outrageous presidential ambitions of his own. These deceitful men worked against all the real problems challenging the American Dream, namely the growing inequality and poverty of the American masses. They worked against one of the most serious problems, affecting all of the human race, overpopulation and the liberation of women and their right to be educated and informed in planning their families.

Presidents Reagan and Bush often rode upon the political bandwagon of the hypocritical millionaires of the religious far right, champions of intolerance, finger pointing, character assassination, hatred, false patriotism, and every other diversion from some serious government reform to produce less waste and more efficiency. The very strong role of religion to influence government encouraged a rise of fascism in American government.

Both Reagan and Bush presided over one of the greatest and most expensive military build-ups in American history, along with the greatest rise in the nation's debt. The American Dream and most of the economic and political progress of the masses were sacrificed by these two presidents, under the pretense of fighting mythical foreign aggression around the world. Both presidents engaged in illegal foreign adventures that may have killed millions of innocent people. Both presidents thumbed their noses at the American congress and operated more like warlords of a barbaric nation than as presidents of a democracy.

A woman psychologist once analyzed President Bush on public television, using both public and private records. The psychologist concluded that George Bush suffered from a terrible personality disorder based upon a long standing jealousy of an over-demanding father. She gave that analysis to explain why Bush demeaned all Americans by lowering himself to the same level as the Iraqi dictator, Saddam Hussein, in their infamous confrontation. George Bush's desperate anxiety to parade as much macho power as Saddam Hussein made him invent his famous words that in the end of his political career would come back to haunt him: "Read my lips." The American people read George Bush's lips wisely enough, and got rid of him as fast as possible, but not before a great deal of harm had been done to the nation.

It is not surprising that in the great turn to the right in American politics, one of the first targets would be public education and all its related media. History shows that no previous American president to George Bush had contradicted himself so much and relied upon sleaze and character assassination in order to gain his office. Bush liked to brag about being a war hero in World War II, but he did not like it to be pointed out that he was a pilot, and it was common for the American upper classes to avoid the real duress of combat in the infantry by becoming a fly boy.

The American Dream had taken such a bad beating under the administrations of both Ronald Reagan and George Bush that even Bush remarked upon it when he sensed his oncoming defeat in the presidential election. He called for a kinder, gentler America after he had done his best to effect the opposite. The United States under Reagan and Bush had taken a completely opposite path to the pursuit of freedom, democracy, disarmament, and independence for the American Dream.

History lies because the historian is only human and cannot possibly interpret accurately, or even faithfully, the truth. Truths are not constants, they change with time and subjectivity.

Ross Perot, the American maverick presidential candidate in 1992, agreed with all those alarmed at the fast disappearing great American Dream. He could entertain his presidential ambitions because he was a multi-millionaire who had made his fortune in insider government contracts within the highly profitable military industrial complex.

Perot had strong opinions about the fast-fading American Dream, but professional experts and think tanks are nearly always dead wrong, as in the case of the sudden collapse of the Soviet Empire.

The experts went overboard in proclaiming a sure peace dividend for the fast-fading great American Dream of the people. Instead, things got rapidly worse with President Bill Clinton's incompetence, and the sudden political rise of the American radical right.

Other factors rose to pit themselves against the great American Dream. The rise of science and technology, globalization, and the increased greed and wastefulness of unlimited competition and consumption.

Globalization speeded up greedy and wasteful human consumption, greatly aided by misused modern science and technology, and wreaking havoc upon the environment.

Poor Ross Perot complained that Americans were becoming consumers instead of producers and a freedom loving people. He complained also of the fast-multiplying wasteful layers of new elite bureaucracies necessitated by globalization.

Ross Perot mourned the fading American Dream, but his solutions were nothing new. They were too much like the same old politics that had caused the problem in the first place.

Winning at all costs, cutthroat competition, the almighty dollar, and unlimited profit motive without social responsibility and globalization hurt the more deserving and honorable people, rather than the least deserving.

It is exactly the more deserving people in human society who want to live more simply in peace and honor without cutting anybody else's throat who are being completely misled by the modern politicians and their false economic and political priorities.

The more modern science and technology become addicted to the false economics of modern politics, the more the human exploiters of society triumph, and the more deserving ordinary people are victimized.

History is the horror tale that man fabricates out of the folly and greed of his false economics. When the Soviet Empire collapsed so suddenly, so did the logic and intelligence of all of modern man's politics in the 20th century. Left wing communists had suddenly become right wing conservatives. True democracy and socialism were out in the cold, and the old folly of nationalism and genocide was back in vogue.

The Cold War had proved to be nothing more than a tragic sham on the poor American people. The great American Dream was dying with the rise of the radical right wing conservatives and the fascism of the moral majority. The peace dividend, long promised to the greatly abused American people, never materialized. The modern American politicians had continued the subjugation of their people by simply replacing the Cold War with globalization.

Modern man's political dignitaries assembled in New York City in 1995 to celebrate the United Nations' 50th anniversary. Ironically, the United States was way behind in paying its dues, but evidently because of its power and bully tactics all around the world, its president was allowed to make the longest speech. The murderous Fidel Castro of Cuba received the greatest ovation. The modern mass media was in all its glory as the politicians confessed and exposed all their strange bedfellows.

Obviously, all the world's leaders were in their greatest glory in their own exclusive club of hypocrites. It was the quickly-fading poor American Dream that became the scapegoat and took the greatest beating. All the dignitaries from around the world were crying and pointing their fingers at the United States, blaming that nation for all their troubles. The solution was simple, the United States and of course the American people, should always pay more and more.

The poor American Dream rolled over and died at this historical meeting. Its own government had spent billions in favor of globalization and getting rid of American workers and replacing them with the slave labor of foreign dictatorships.

The main culprit in slave labor was China, that reportedly had strong words with the weakling American president, Bill Clinton, who was suddenly showing some humanitarian concern for the results of globalization.

Interestingly enough, China enjoyed special preferential treatment among nations trading with the United States. Bill Clinton was a Democrat. The American president who had engineered China's special status was the Republican Richard Nixon. Small wonder that the American people had lost all trust in their political system.

The American president who opened up the floodgate that destroyed the American Dream was the mass media's great favorite, Ronald Reagan. When Bill Clinton was just a presidential candidate, he declared that the massacre of the people of East Timor, by the ruthless dictator of Indonesia should not be tolerated. When Bill Clifton became president, he was meeting with the bloodthirsty dictator, Suharto, still killing the same innocent people, but better armed with sophisticated American weapons of war.

The 50th anniversary of the United Nations showed off the full extent of modern man's corrupted leadership. It was suggested to increase the number of nations in the Security Council. It was not a very well kept secret that only a few wealthy nations actually control the United Nations, and that had been the case right from the start of the organization. East Timor was just one of the hundreds of great shams perpetuated in the halls of the U.N. The cowardly men with the guns still controlled the world and their corrupted whims were forced upon the weaker nations.

Some of the American presidential candidates in 1995 were Bob Dole, Phil Graham, Steve Forbes, Pat Buchanan, Lamar Alexander, and others, including Ross Perot and even Colin Powell. The real qualifications of these people were that they simply had the best chances of accumulating enough finances in order to satisfy their lusts for political power. Real intelligence and ability came in last as requirements for the ambitious, and those lusting for the power and the status of the office.

Both Forbes and Buchanan had made their considerable fortunes as professionals in the mass media.

Strangely enough, only a few years before 1995, both presidents Reagan and Bush complained that the American mass media was too liberal. That situation seemed to have been reversed by 1995, with the two right wing radical Republican candidates for president, Buchanan and Forbes, both emanating from the nation's powerful mass media.

In a moment of candor and honesty, Pat Buchanan did admit that he had seen no legitimate excuse for the American led Persian Gulf War. The American Dream itself seemed to have collapsed in the stark immorality of that war.

All the candidates in the peculiar American presidential election campaign of 1995 seemed to agree that the nation's political system was on the verge of complete bankruptcy. This was no surprise to the vast majority of the American people who had been witnessing for so long its sad decline.

The people knew long before their so-called political leaders that their nation and their great American Dream was in dire danger of collapse.

The Hoax in the Persian Gulf

In the Persian Gulf, Iraq is reported to be close to the cradle of civilization. Throughout human history, man has been trying to lift himself above his savage state, and Iraq no doubt has often been an important stage to his efforts. In modern times Iraq had become more important to the major industrial nations because of its large oil reserves, even though it was suffering from a volatile instability common to the Middle East and the struggle for individual human rights against the various sects of Islam.

In 1990, the United States was the top superpower in the world and it had no problem leading a lightning swift war against Iraq and its berserk dictator, Saddam Hussein. As in previous actions of this type, the American superpower sought and received the full support of most of the United Nations. The American public opinion was won over to the war rather easily by fabricating an imaginative and rather fictitious scenario of the nation's innocence and the great threat that Saddam Hussein and Iraq was to American national security.

The war was quick and swift, but Saddam Hussein remained in power to continue his murderous ways, and the American people woke up daily to new information about the war. The

Persian Gulf War has to go down in American history as the greatest hoax ever created by the government to deceive the people. Even the American mass media finally complained how they had been muzzled and kept far away from the truth.

In 1992, the American people took vengeance on President George Bush the self-proclaimed hero of the Persian Gulf War, by electing Bill Clinton. The people knew there had been a hoax in the Gulf War, but worse was the decline in the quality of their life.

An entire book could be written about the buyout and the control of the American mass media, and the ease with which the government can lie. Before the Persian Gulf War, both Bush and Reagan were deeply implicated in covert actions in support of Saddam Hussein and Iraq against the much larger and more feared Iran. It took many years before the details of these often illegal operations in favor of Iraq against Iran became known to the American public. The consciences of the two American presidents Bush and Reagan never seemed to have been bothered much in their acts of international terrorism.

Forgetting all his plotting and participation in support of Iraq against Iran, George Bush suddenly turned against Saddam Hussein in 1990, when he occupied Kuwait and threatened Saudi Arabia. An immediate controversy arose as to whether the United States had not encouraged Hussein's aggression against his neighbors in the Middle East.

After a thorough congressional investigation that has been kept quite well-hidden from the American public, it was concluded that the great blunderer in Iraq's occupation of Kuwait may have been Bush himself with the help of the incompetent Ambassador to Iraq, April Glaspie. Some major American senators on the Foreign Relations Committee were stunned by the incompetence of the president's and his ambassador's official messages to Saddam Hussein, when he made it so clear that he intended to occupy Kuwait. The senators listened to some official tapes of the American government that seemed to condone an Iraqi invasion of Kuwait.

On February 11, nearly a month after the Americans led the land invasion of Iraq, Secretary of State Baker shocked the world with an alarming confession. He said, "Maybe-yes, absolutely," as to whether the U.S. could have prevented the Persian Gulf War if it had better handled its diplomacy with Iraq. There is no longer any doubt that President Bush and his top aides were blinded by their hereto friendly relationship with Saddam Hussein. Their blundering helped cause a war that could have been avoided, killing thousands of innocent Iraqi civilians, many more than their soldiers.

Fortunately for the United States, Saddam Hussein may have been one of the greatest military fools in history. After barely surviving his long war with Iran, he evidently had started to believe in his own invincibility. Like any dictator with too many weapons at his disposal, he was foolhardy, but not fool enough to have invaded Kuwait without a strong conviction that the friendly American president in the White House would make a little noise, but look the other way. For years, the freedom-loving people in the Arab world wanted to get rid of the corrupt royal families of both Kuwait and Saudi Arabia.

As soon as Saddam Hussein realized his great mistake in trusting George Bush to remain complacent, he panicked and worried only about his own survival as lord and master of his own people. He withdrew his best troops out of harm's way to protect his own power. Not only did he survive George Bush as the leader of his nation, but he also rose up again to terrorize and kill any Shiites and Kurds who had believed in some American support for their aspirations for freedom.

When reading about the Persian Gulf War in future history

books, there will be very little mention about any of the American people's opposition to it. The nation's mass media kept pretending that all Americans were happy in bombing and killing thousands of innocent Iraqi civilians. Nothing will be written about the hundreds of organizations and thousands of Americans who stood up against the war, nor anything will be said about the more than fifty American military personnel who refused to serve in the Gulf. Both Patrick Buchanan, a later right wing Republican candidate for president, and Tom Wicker, a respected columnist for the New York Times newspaper, came out against the war.

The opposition to the Persian Gulf War was based very simply upon morality, that singular entity that seems so beyond the modern-day politician's understanding. Too much power corrupts one and all. Give a man a gun and he will soon turn into a savage and become a coward. Give the cowardly man high technology weapons with mass killing potential, and he will surely find an excuse to use them, even if he has to kill more women and children than soldiers. The Council of American Churches declared that the Persian Gulf War was immoral. President Bush though, was anxious to cover up both his and Ronald Reagan's role in covert American foreign military operations.

The war went forward, starting with the American saturation bombing of Baghdad, where too many of the targets were of the civilian infrastructure. This was a time of the greatest shame in American history. It was the false use of American military power to control foreign oil supplies that did not belong to the United States.

War is a complete breakdown in man's already fragile intelligence. Too often the winner of wars becomes the loser in the long run. Very often it is the cream of the crop in the nation who die in its wars, leaving only the misfits to survive. These misfits help form history's continuing horror tale, especially those who lust for power. Violence always harms democracy and freedom.

It is the ordinary man, the more honest man, the poor gullible sap who has to fight the wars for his demented leaders. Ordinary people are so much more used to sacrificing themselves for others than most of the power hungry leaders of the world. Democracies that declare wars have to do a terrific amount of lying in order to justify the upcoming slaughter of the innocent. George Bush, having adopted the lowest road of character assassination just to gain the presidency of the United States, only showed how low he was willing to stoop in his unquenchable lust for power.

Bill Moyers of the Public Broadcasting System gave a completely opposite opinion about the morality of the Gulf War than George Bush. Needless to say that the opinion was not very flattering to George Bush, and at least not all Americans were fooled by their nation's propaganda favoring the war.

Former President Eisenhower had warned about the immorality of a very expensive Military Industrial Complex. The war in the Gulf was an economic bonanza for every exotic weapon's system in the American military arsenal. The exaggerations on the perfect performance of these weapons were quickly discredited by the reality of their breakdown in the field. The innocent people killed did not seem to count much.

"Rescue Bridgeport, Connecticut, not Kuwait," cried a 70-year-old handicapped woman who had been mugged twice in her native city. She and hundreds of other protesters against the war were harassed and attacked in their peace march between Bridgeport and Norwalk, Connecticut. Violence in their own cities remained much more dangerous for American citizens than for those among them who would serve in the Persian Gulf War.

No other people would have had the good luck of facing a

military leader as incompetent as Saddam Hussein. "Why, the man was downright crazy," most people proclaimed, after they were presented the facts of the war. Two women reporters wrote a book about Saddam Hussein's military folly, proclaiming that any ordinary housewife could have used Iraq's army more efficiently.

A new look at the war shows why so many American veterans of World War II and other real wars become so insulted at the hoax in the Persian Gulf. The war took 268 American lives and it was described by the Bush administration as a good, clean, and humane war. It was also known as the first television war. American generals were seen with pointers and maps, bragging about the surgical precision of their smart bombs until their faces turned red when errant bombs hit civilian hospitals and air raid shelters, killing thousands of innocent women and children.

Some old-timer veterans of war call the Pursian Gulf War the Mutt and Jeff War, enabling them to laugh instead of cry in shame. A Harvard study team concluded that it was nearly impossible to count all the Iraqi casualties of war, and that economic sanctions would only hurt the innocent.

Three Catholic priests from Fairfield University, spoke out against the Gulf War, putting forth their arguments for the real reasons for the war. The president of the nation, the politicians, and the people all agreed that there was a deep economic recession in 1990, and that the national infrastructure was falling apart through government neglect. Not only highway bridges were falling down, but crime and social problems were out of control. To make matter even worse, Ronald Reagan's induced Savings and Loan scandal was depressing the whole nation. The war was heaven-sent for the crooked politicians to get themselves off the hook.

Granada, Panama, Kuwait, and Iraq only delayed the tide and turmoil of the American social, political, and economic problems that finally exploded in civil unrest, riots, vandalism, and violence all over the nation in 1992. International military adventures gained national self-respect and international prestige that made it much easier to hide the real problems of the nation.

The best kept American secret since World War II has been the high cost and social burden of keeping such a ridiculously large armed forces at the ready in peacetime. American soldiers were spread out all over the world, and it was ridiculous to think that such a huge army can be kept forever in peacetime without some very serious consequences to the nation. Neither the president nor the politicians who use the American Armed Forces for their own glory were likely to ever tell the truth about the devastating waste and the economic burden to the nation.

The United States was accumulating so much military hardware that it was literally running out of room to store it. Ever since the nation's defense industry had gained so much power over the economy, there was too little room for any other interest. The more the Great American Dream evaporated, the more the young and the desperate from the lower economic segment of the population flocked to the armed forces. Even women sought out the military life for the same equity and free handouts as the men, but tripling the cost to the taxpayers. The American military became a huge boondoggle of a lunatic social experiment with one of the largest orphanages in the world for all the children of mothers who did not particularly want them.

Nearly all the American propaganda about the great success of the Persian Gulf War was just that—mere propaganda and not very true. The Smart Bombs were not smart at all. Many of them were not even new, they were from old storage facilities, all around the world and not very accurate. None of the great hype about the wonderful efficiency of the American Patriot missiles given to Israel to protect that nation against the crude Iraqi Scud missiles was true either.

Several later military analysis reports accused the American Patriot missiles of having actually increased the terror and devastation caused by the Iraqi Scud missiles, by increasing a wider area of lethal falling debris. Not only was there the great disgrace of a high number of American military women killed in the Gulf War, but the Pentagon admitted that 35 out of the 148 Americans killed in the war were victims of friendly fire.

Obviously, the Persian Gulf War, like most wars, was a fiasco with none of the soldiers and none of the weapons working as well as expected or as claimed by the government. It is rare that any army ever does live up to expectations, and the Americans were no different than anybody else. In the quickly changing military situation in modern times, the armies of superpowers have proven too often to be nothing more than overblown and very expensive big white elephants.

Haste, inefficiency, and a terrible lack of discipline under fire led to the tragic toll of Allied troops to friendly fire. British parents of English soldiers killed by American fire later sued the American government for economic compensation.

The greatest shame was not all the American women killed in the war, but the great cowardice of President George Bush in saving the Iraqi dictator's neck, breaking his vow to remove Saddam Hussein from power. President Bush termed his reasons as political, but they proved to be irresponsible and cynical as Saddam Hussein rose again to indiscriminately slay all his former political foes.

The cynical politics of a superpower had turned a victory obtained in an unjust and unforgivable war into a major national shame and a defeat for democracy around the world. The United States was obviously more interested in globalization, the almighty dollar, and its growing consumption of Middle Eastern oil that it was in the promotion of democracy worldwide.

Globalization

E ven the dictionary does not seem to know exactly what globalization means, especially in its new worldwide economic and political sense. Before globalization, there was great colonial empires trying to put the whole world, and as many of its people they could conquer, under their own despotic rule. After globalization, the colonial despotic rule of the world moved into the halls of the United Nations with the rich nations and the superpowers holding the upper hand. Modern science and technology, with their massive destructive weapons, aided the intimidation of the rich and the powerful nations over the poor and the destitute nations. A whole new world was being formed, but the same lust for power and greed still burned in the breasts of an exclusive elite.

Globalization crept up into man's world during World War II and has been growing ever since. It has been greatly helped and speeded up by the misuse and misdirection of modern science and technology. It is fueled by the economic greed and the lust for power of entrenched elites from many nations. It encourages unlimited human consumption with endless economic expansion that can only lead to ecological damage to the whole world. It is but another form of determined, closed-minded, and sometimes fanatic attempt to dominate nearly every aspect of human life.

Globalization is not an American invention. It is more the

economic invention of an obscure foreign economist by the name of Jean Monet. The globalization that grew so rapidly after World War II, had managed to turn around the great victory of the United States in that war to a resounding defeat.

Too often human ideas evolve so that they no longer resemble their original forms or intentions. The American political leaders who entered WW II to save democracy and freedom had no premonition that their nation would go overboard becoming a superpower and a policeman of the world who would so often side with tyrants against freedom and democracy.

What appeared at first to be such an ingenuous idea of helping Saddam Hussein of Iraq in his war against a much more feared Iran, turned eventually into the holocaust of the Persian Gulf War, killing thousands of completely innocent people. So many apparently good human ideas end in disasters. Soviet dictated communism seems to have been in that category, and globalization could turn out that way too.

The disgraced American president, Richard Nixon, certainly should have known that by opening the doors of globalization to the cruel dictatorship of China he was condemning millions of Chinese to slave labor.

Globalization was maybe fortunately delayed by the long idiotic Cold War. Any fool learns quickly that what he can accomplish peacefully will be more creative and enduring than whatever he tries by violence. If the world's leaders had listened to President Dwight Eisenhower who refused to use force on several occasions, the cause of peace and progress in the world could have been much more advanced.

Instead, the demented leaders of the world real or imagined superpowers, continued to rattle their swords at each other, and assembled in the halls of the United Nations to celebrate their folly.

Both Presidents Eisenhower and Kennedy predicted that man can never progress until he stopped using war to settle political disputes. Both Ronald Reagan and George Bush seemed busier in foreign aggression than in their own nation's welfare. Reagan and Bush attacked the welfare of the American middle class and the workingman with unprecedented viciousness. Ronald Reagan's Great Recession did the nation's middle class more harm than President Herbert Hoover's Great Depression in the 1930s.

Reaganomics was the beginning of the end for the Great American Dream. It was the start of globalization, asking countless millions of Americans to give up their productive careers, and lower all their future expectations in the service of globalization. Ronald Reagan got the corporate controlled mass media to play up his popularity by offering the people extravagant tax cuts. A whole new wave of crooked politicians sprung up in the nations, offering the American people tax cuts, even though the United States was one of the least taxed among all the rich and developed nations.

The American people were hoodwinked each time another dishonest politician offered a tax cut in exchange for a seat of power. As their local taxes and usage fees escalated, they soon found out that their tax cuts were mostly myths, and they lost their employment to globalization by the millions. More underhanded than anything else in the entrenchment of globalization, was the skyrocketing salaries and golden parachutes handed out to corporate managers, even when these same managers were sending millions of American workers packing without any realistic prospects for the future. The age of extortion of the American manager and the nation's political process was on its way.

Some ideas turn out differently from what was intended before they were put into practice. Soviet communism became more a vehicle to advance the special privileges of the communist party elite than it was ever a truly egalitarian social system.

Globalization was also bound to turn out very differently from its original intentions. The elite of every nation must view globalization as just another opportunity for the privileged to exploit the ordinary people.

As modern man makes his life forever more complicated, he creates endless new opportunities for his own exploitation, by new bureaucracies and their hierarchies. Some of the worst exploiters may have been vicious tyrants or terrorists, before they assembled together in the halls of the United Nations to celebrate their glory.

Globalization may produce the exact opposite results than what was intended, because it has to be refined and defined by too many different institutions with their bureaucracies and hierarchies. Globalization may easily become yet another huge welfare program for the rich and the elite.

The trouble with globalization was that whether it was a good idea or not, it had to become institutionalized and thus corrupted. At the same time, little thought had been given to its morality. History shows how disastrous some of man's institutionalized ideas have been.

Globalization was the beginning of the end of the Great American Dream. It attacked humanism and individualism at every turn. It gave too much power to the overeducated fools in professional think tanks. The too simplistic formulation of globalization was more profitable to the cruel tyrannies of nations like China and Indonesia, while it victimized too many democracies and squelched the chances of alleviating the widespread starvation existing in underdeveloped nations.

Globalization seemed to have been already well on its way when President George Bush declared a New World Order. Its urgency and destructiveness accelerated under the misguidance of the dishonest politicians and other human exploiters. Another tier of wasteful hierarchies with new elites had been created to subdue democracy and individualism.

While the politicians and the new elites were the main beneficiaries of globalization, countless millions of people around the world were victimized. They were forced to abandon their traditional economic opportunities and crafts that had been handed down to them from generation to generation.

As naive and gullible man was giving more and more power to fewer and fewer men, the ordinary man, the workingman, the middle class, and the individual were suffering more and more. In American politics the scenario became perfect for the rise of cruel radical right wing conservatism.

The vast majority of the American people woke up suddenly to find out that their political system was completely bypassing all their best interests. Globalization seemed to have contaminated their precious two major political party system. The infiltration of both the Democrats and Republicans by the super rich, the bankers, and the corporate merger buffs made both major political parties completely enthralled with globalization, and absolutely unresponsive to the average American citizen's normal everyday interest.

The dormant American mass media, fallen more and more into the hands of corporate mergers that naturally favored globalization, finally woke up to the reality of the widespread political discontent of the vast majority of the American people. Finally, some of the political fallout was discussed more thoroughly, and the nation could realize the seriousness of the abyss and predicament in the fast-fading American Dream.

The American Booksellers Association, very much associated with globalization and the corporate world as well as its pretended interest in literature, unwittingly exposed the ruling political dilemma when it promoted two contrasting books of its fantasy candidates for president, Colin Powell and Newt Gingrich in 1995. Both men were truly fantasy candidates for the presidency, because it was so advantageous to the mass media to declare it. Colin Powell had become a mass media star after another general in the Persian Gulf War, Norman Scharzkopf, faded from the limelight. Colin Powell was black, good-looking, and eloquent, and a perfect prize for commercial exploitation. Powell had been chairman for the Joint Chiefs of Staff in the Persian Gulf War.

The other mass media's fantasy candidate was no other than the radical new Republican Speaker of the House, Newt Gingrich, a former history teacher at West Georgia College. Mr. Gingrich had arrived at the top, through the usual blasphemy and jealous infighting that had become so normal in modern American politics.

General Colin L. Powell was still a gentleman and very undecided about facing the widespread dishonesty so prevalent in a political career. The contrast between the two fantasy candidates was both startling and clear. One was not a politician yet, and he was still honest, while the other one was a fully baptized loud-mouthed politician, basking in self-importance.

All the popularity polls went overboard naturally favoring Powell over Gingrich. Unfortunately, Colin Powell woke up one day soon after, and still finding honest bones left in his body, he rejected his inside track to his nation's presidency.

The dunces in the White House do not get there through merit and honesty, without huge destructive egos and lusts for power. The miracle is that the nation survives with the low caliber of men who creep and crawl into the White House, and all that globalization has accomplished is to make the fate of the average American less opportune when it could have still been pursuing the Great American Dream.

General Colin L. Powell had such an inside track to the American presidency because the vast majority of the people were completely disgusted with the nation's politicians, and they realized that neither major political party had any honest concern whatsoever with the best interest of the average American citizen. Many politicians with honesty still left within them were leaving politics in droves.

The runaway ideas that produced globalization have caused more than just the destruction of the Great American Dream, the pursuit of democracy, and the validity of the American two major political parties' system, but they have created many other dangerous consequences, completely unforeseen by the ego-driven pundits that dreamed them up.

Some of the original dreamers of globalization claimed that it would encourage free enterprise and individual capitalism, and thus promote political freedom and democracy. Much was being said about free markets, when no such thing has ever existed, even in the most laissez-faire democratic atmosphere of uncluttered capitalism.

Man is a greedy animal and unfair advantages are always sought after. Small wonder that globalization has best benefited the tyrannies of China and Indonesia whose cost of government is so small when compared to any full-blown democracy. The free enterprise in these fast growing economies are tightly controlled by a few powerful families and cliques. These nations are not above using convenient slave labor to propel all their advantages over democracies. The powerful families and cliques control their governments.

Obviously, globalization has put great strains upon all democratic governments and their high costs, but even worse it is killing free enterprise and individual capitalism in any nation, where the vast majority of the people want to safeguard their democracy and political freedom.

Already the trend to redistribute the wealth in the United States became notable in the 1980s when more and more small enterprises folded and gave way to huge corporate jealousy and greed.

Huge and frequent corporate mergers were changing the American free enterprise system, destroying individual capitalism, and endangering democracy, all for the sake of playing the power and greed games of globalization. Corporate capitalism resembled more the old failed central Soviet communist economic system than it resembled any true individual democratic capitalistic system. Globalization was obviously forming a huge welfare system for the rich and the powerful at the expense of democracy.

Another horror of globalization was the obvious increase in economic competition between nations, resulting most surely in more wasteful and ecologically disastrous consumption. History is full of the doomsayers who keep predicting man's early demise, caused presumably by his own consumption and greed. When President John F. Kennedy created the American Space Agency to compete against the Soviet Union, he never dreamed that one day the American people would be forced to financially support both nations' very expensive and wasteful space agencies.

The doomsayers are not always right, because man often wakes up to reality when he feels his back against the wall. Some of the over-educated fools who had been promoting nuclear energy worldwide woke up to its dangers when Chernobyl blew up causing the end of the Soviet Union's empire. The Soviet demise may have been aided by its compulsion to compete with other nations economically with globalization and the necessity of economic expansion, consumption, and industrialization. Modern man, with all his globalization so speeded up by his science and technology, has nearly no idea where it all will lead him to.

There is no doubt that globalization has meant a loss of national independence and soul for the American people.

Losing Mind

Another great contrast between the two fantasy presidential candidates, General Colin L. Powell and Newt Gingrich, presented at the Booksellers Convention, was the great difference in their minds. One was an enthusiastic optimist and the other was an unabashed destructive pessimist, even though both men professed their allegiance to the same Republican political party.

A modest General Colin L. Powell credited the greatness of the United States for having encouraged him to rise to the top of his profession after a rather humble beginning in the mean streets of the Bronx. He also praised the strength and character of his parents.

Newt Gingrich had a completely opposite mind about the greatness of his nation. He spewed venom left and right, and talked very little about his teaching career in a small Georgia College, saying nearly nothing about how he had clawed his way to the top of his new political profession.

The same Republican political party was exhibiting two remarkably different minds in what was supposed to be the same political forum. It was the optimist against the pessimist, it was the liberal against the conservative, but the more affable and reasonable Colin Powell preferred to be regarded as a middle of the road, while the more arrogant Newt Gingrich was extremely proud to be viewed as an extremely radical conservative.

Needless to say, that the vast majority of Americans and most intelligent people, march in the middle of the road, searching for the reasonable path. Colin Powell had to march that way because he was a reasonable man and a self-made man. He was so reasonable that he soon decided that he was too honest to play the hypocritical game of dirty politics.

Newt Gingrich knew very well that the United States was not a democracy, and that political power very rarely rested in the hands of honest, self-made men. As a former history teacher, he knew that less and less American voters had been voting in presidential elections ever since the 1960s. He knew exactly where he had come from and who had paid the way for him to reach his outlandish position of power as the Speaker of the House.

Newt Gingrich was an extremely arrogant and ambitious man and did not hide his very definite presidential ambitions. He knew that his greatest strength was the unlimited financial support of the rising tide of radical conservative bankrollers in the United States. He also knew that his greatest liability was his own abrasive personality and that there was always other more pleasing personalities with strong presidential ambitions that his radical right wing backers would more likely support for president.

Newt Gingrich was truly the pathetic figure of the modern American politician. He was a mere mouthpiece of the best organized and bankrolled entity in the Republican political party. He could be thrown to the wolves at any time his backers would decide. Unfortunately for the nation, the more Newt Gingrich became desperate to retain his political power, the more he lost the mind of a conservative and the more he gained the mind of a radical destroyer.

Power corrupts one and all and too much power corrupts

even more. As Newt Gingrich seemed to obviously be losing his mind, the powers behind him stirred uneasily. Different feelers were sent out to the pathetic Speaker of the House, reminding him of his subservience.

In modern times, the American politicians who are elected to office assume much greater power than was intended for them by the nation's constitution. They do not serve the people, they only serve themselves; and the mass media plays along with their silly political demagoguery because it helps sell newspapers.

Newt Gingrich confessed that he had deliberately written a budget stopgag measure that he knew the president would reject, in revenge for a lack of courtesy shown to him on an airplane ride to Israel for the funeral of that nation's assassinated Prime Minister, Yitzhak Rabin.

The confession was made at the time the President of the United States had to close down many government operations for budgetary reasons in silly political games, creating havoc in the lives of millions of people. The event underlined the complete bankruptcy of the nation's whole political system. The American people were supposed to pay the price of the folly of two spoiled political demagogues, having ego problems on an airplane ride to a distant land, where the necessity of their presence was very questionable.

The confession and the spectacle of two grown men with too much power each, were enough to make most of the American people lose their minds. They had to pay their bills and their government did not. The people they elected could spend their money at the slightest whim and temper tantrum. And worse of all, they had absolutely no choice between the fully displayed corruption shown by both of their major political parties. Politicians, like the Speaker of the House and the President of the United States, were interested only in self-glorification.

Newt Gingrich had not become the mouthpiece of the right by accident, but with the backing of several formidable conservative political brainwashing organizations, one of which was called Heritage Foundation, under the direction of a rather famed New Right activist by the name of Paul Weyrich.

Gingrich and Weyrich certainly had unlimited funding behind them from dozens of pressure groups, attacking and controlling the nation's freedom of the press and the mass media. With great discipline and the generous financial support of super rich philanthropists such as Joseph Coors, a beer magnate, and Richard Mellon Scaife from a great banking family, the extremism of the right wing conservatives grew more and more radical.

As Gingrich's and Weyrich's power and success grew, they departed further and further away from truly traditional conservative dispositions and creeds. They were truly forming an attack machine that was going out of control in their lust for power, and threatened the whole American democratic charade, still left standing in the nation's political system. When men gather up too much power they forget all about their professions and creeds—their hypocrisy rules.

According to professor Clinton Rossiter in his book on conservatism in America, a true conservative is always a moderate and never an extremist. True conservatism is also a thankless persuasion, never soliciting huge rewards for its sober, prudent, and cautious views. A true conservative usually comes out of the middle class or a comfortable but modest financial segment of the nation's population. A true conservative is more reactionary than he is ever a radical.

The true conservative pursues social stability—he even begs for it—because he is afraid of the chaos of sudden change. Even though he knows that change is inevitable, he wants to study it and is cautious about it. The true conservative knows the limitations of his thankless persuasion, and he allows that most of the progressive changes in society will emerge from the mind of his alter ego, the liberal.

Rossiter, the respected guru of American conservatism, emphasizes that no truly intelligent man can ever be either all conservative or all liberal. For him though, it was more conservative than liberal, and he admitted that without the liberal, the conservative could not exist.

Gingrich and Weyrich were not conservatives, they were extremists and destroyers of democracy, spewing hate, intolerance, and ridicule around the nation.

Right wing extremism is usually more prone to violence than left wing extremism, but they are both equally destructive. The conservative does have the bad habit of coddling the aristocracy and the elite more than the liberal because he lusts so much to be considered part of the elite.

Most of the American people are in the middle of the political spectrum in favor of democracy, and they are sick and tired of the obnoxious debate between the conservative and the liberal that has destroyed all semblance of good government and all honesty in politics.

The American people would like solutions to social and economic injustice, and they seriously question the wisdom of big business, giant corporate mergers and the lunatic salaries of their officers, while they remain so ignored by the political establishment in its horrendous mismanagement of the nation.

The spectacle of the dishonest American politician is disheartening, both in the White House and at the local level. Widespread social and economic malaise grows in every corner of a once proud and honorable nation.

Neither of the major political parties in the United States is addressing the real problems of the people and the declining index in the quality of their lives.

Neither political party has questioned the morality of big business, giant corporate mergers, globalization, the attack against individual free enterprise, the unlimited greed of science and technology, or any other important questions that could slow down the growing tragic economic disparity between the rich and the poor in the nation.

Neither political party has moved against the outlandish rape of the wealth of the nation by the exclusive club of chief corporate officers and all other sick and greedy hoarders of wealth who are ruining all the best chances of democracy and human progress in the nation.

Snake Pits and False Heroes

History lies, true democracy has never existed, and all the pretending democracies have their snake pits and false heroes. History is not the great teacher it pretends to be. It is usually the neo-conservative who writes it, but most often it is the liberal and the radical who make history.

Conservatism can be insidious, and the best kept secret in the history of the United States is its political mainstream ambition to dominate the nation. Once again Ronald Reagan was the president with the weak mind who allowed the extremist groups of the religious right in the United States to gain too much political power, threatening the whole nation's democracy.

Ronald Reagan made history because he was such a great destroyer of the American Dream. The distance between him and a true conservative, such as the father of modern American conservatism, Senator Barry Goldwater of Arizona, was more than a million miles.

Ronald Reagan was never a true conservative, interested in a more honest and efficient government. His whole political career was as a great destroyer of good government. He made a mockery out of his own nation's laws, both domestically and internationally, but he was still able to retain the moronic adoration of the nation's mass media.

Reganomics was one of the most horrendous economic disasters any nation has endured in history, because it was so totally unnecessary. Ronald Reagan's bank scandals and his vicious attacks against organized labor spelled the end of a long period of human progress in the United States. His runaway increase in the nation's debt was unforgivable.

Ronald Reagan's pathetic reverence for England's Prime Minister, Margaret Thatcher, was disastrous. They were both darlings of the mass media, and connived together to bankroll international corporate moguls and hustlers, both in the mass media and the international armament sales business. They caused thousands of their own countrymen to lose their social and economic security.

Ronald Reagan's covert armament sales around the world was shameful, and surely caused thousands of innocent people to die unnecessarily. The United States helped preserve the arrogance of the fast-fading British Empire in its struggle to retain ownership of the Falkland Islands against Argentina. The United States, under Reagan, helped retain many bloodthirsty tyrants around the world.

Ronald Reagan always pretended to court the American workingman, while always doing the contrary. He stabbed the workingman and the middle class in the back as soon as he managed to become president. He catered to the rich while the nation's parks, government services, and infrastructure deteriorated in front of everybody's eyes. The rich, of course, never suffered because they were getting richer much faster than expected, and could easily afford their own services.

The average American did not find out what had hit him until it was far too late. The freedom of speech was effectively curtailed, with the mass media and government misinformation rampant throughout the nation by the time of the Persian Gulf War.

The American people never found out that they were the only advanced wealthy nation in the world without any normal health, education, or social security.

Corporate executives were being made into false heroes by the nation's boot licking mass media. Many of them were belatedly caught in one fraud or another, and quite a few were sent to prison for their grand larceny against both people and entire nations. The honesty of Wall Street and the entire financial world was being questioned and severely doubted.

Some of the corporate executives survived all the scrutiny, but too many were tainted. Some, like Bill Gates of Microsoft Corporation traveled around the world and were received like royalty. Unfortunately for the average people of many of those nations, the American message that these false heroes were spreading, meant gloom, doom, and future misery for the vast majority of them.

The message was clear. The new world order, devised by American big business, was not above blackmailing the economic health of other nations. The American corporate executives flaunted their close association with their nation's political establishment and its military might. These false heroes and ugly diplomats were not bluffing as they waved the greatly dishonored flag of the United States of America.

The message was preaching all the snake pits of globalization and a new world order that would greatly benefit a new American sanctioned worldwide elite at the expense of the ordinary middle class and working people of the world.

Free markets would be fine as long as they were supervised by the United States. Other nations were given little choice but to buckle down and embrace the American plan of speed and greed with unlimited consumption and economic expansion worldwide.

American diplomacy worldwide had never been famous for its intelligence nor its education and knowledge of other nations. Economic sanctions were part of the new international blackmail.

While the United States was paying for the lion's share of becoming the world's prime policeman, their own people's quality of life was falling behind many other more intelligent rich nations. The American elite relished its role of world leadership, and the elite of other nations took full advantage of the American gullibility. The only losers were the vast majority of the American people.

The nation's infrastructure was declining so quickly, and the government's deficit escalating likewise, that the dishonest and desperate American politicians had to resort to gambling and state lotteries to cover up their folly. The cost of armaments and the welfare programs for the rich multiplied at the same time that sane social security programs were being squeezed out.

The degenerate American politician had managed to completely change the direction of his nation's historical devotion to human progress and the development of true democracy. Most American citizens did not even know that their presidential election and their vote for a president was more mirage than fact since it could conceivably be overturned by the electoral college vote.

Stunning revelations of the dealings of a small time minion in the White House, by the name of Oliver North, showed how exactly berserk a president of the United States and its government could become.

Newt Gingrich and Paul Weyrich, the patron of the American Conservative radical right, knew full well how corrupted the American political system had become. They pointed the finger at the president just because he was from another party, but they lusted for the same corrupted power.

The American mass media often seems to be the only entity

not fully aware of what is going on, either in their country, or worldwide. It is as if it is too much to ask to just report the news as it occurs without spending so many wasteful hours embellishing and distorting it. The result is that other nations manage to cover more news in 20 minutes than the American news services provide in three hours.

Americans may very well be among the most misinformed, and least informed people in the advanced free world. American news services have to sensationalize and fantasize all their stories in order to better satisfy the greedy profit motive of their masters. They seem to invent trivial stories to fill in space, and their world news is anything but.

Love it or leave it. These are often the words yelled at every dissenting opinion, often followed by intimidation and violence. Destroying varying opinion and the spread of fear, are the most commonly used weapons for squelching democracy. Becoming the world's prime policemen of the world was the first step in turning back democracy, and becoming just another imperialistic power. The Americans, who serve in the armed forces and do most of the dirty work as prime policeman of the world, nearly all come from the lower economic segment of the nation. The American presidents, who had become champions of military action in foreign lands, were nearly all afraid of the National Rifle Association and its financial support. Small wonder that some of these presidents thought it was normal for Americans to tote submachine guns around the nation's streets.

The snake pits of inequalities were spreading like wildfire throughout most of the American society.

If anything, history proves that runaway capitalism can serve the purpose of tyranny even better than the causes of democracy. Reaganomics increased—tenfold—the corruption of the American economic system. A simpleminded president had dishonest simpleminded economic and political gimmicks to appeal to the nation's political establishment in order to seek their favor and get himself elected president.

During Reagan's years and ever since, the economic disparity and injustice has grown in the United States by leaps and bounds. As the American economy grows more unequal, the wealthy politicians keep promising more and more tax cuts just to get elected. This should, in all logic, automatically disqualify them from holding office. The arrogance of such a promise is too enormous, and nearly all tax cuts in the United States have always meant extra benefits for the rich, and nothing or even less for the poor.

By all economic reports, the inequality between rich and poor in the United States, reached a 60-year high, thanks to President Ronald Reagan. The American mass media had a tremendous role in creating this false hero and promoting the resulting snake pits.

Yesterday's folly of omitting absolutely essential government reforms to preserve and develop the nation's democracy, has cost the American people dearly. The quality of life for the American family was cut in half between the 1960s and the 1990s. Other nations seem less afraid than the United States to change their constitutions, reform their governments, and improve their democracies.

The United States is falling flat on its face in its pathetic eagerness to become the world's prime superpower.

Tragically, the American mass media, with most of the nation's misused science and technology, help create the pitfalls and false heroes that destroy democracy.

Thousands of brilliant scientists with their technological inventions that serve only the good of man, improving the quality of his life, are completely ignored by the mass media, and they get only a few lines of recognition in obituaries. The biggest headlines in the mass media always seem reserved for the idiots who love the see their names in print.

The vast majority of the American people have watched—in horror—their nation decline in false economic, political, and social priorities, both domestically and on the international scene.

The greatest American snakepit is the unwavering determination of the president dunces in the White House in becoming the world's prime policemen.

Constant greedy economic growth, without due respect for the environment, is a threat to democracy, just like the American founding fathers predicted. That is what finally destroyed the Soviet Union.

Stepping
Backward

Progress has a life of its own in spite of stupid man. History tells the truth about modern man in the 20th century. He has traveled further backward than forward. Modern man is a lightweight intellectual whose hasty thinking and great dependence on artificial intelligence makes him so dangerous to himself and his environment.

For nearly 100 years, modern man has made no significant social, economic, or political progress. The only thing he can brag about is his rapid development of science and technology which he has managed so badly, that it has become potentially suicidal.

Modern man shows his stupidity when he abandons centuries-old progressive ideas in favor of some simpleminded dictates emanating from his artificial intelligence. He has thus created an elite ruling class of experts, more in self-deception than strong in any virtue.

Capitalism is nothing new and has been in place since the minting of coin and the Roman Empire days. It has been mostly a gross failure, and the only time that it is successful is when it manages to equitably serve the greatest majority of the people as possible. It has enjoyed all too few years of good conduct because it is too easily dominated by human vice rather than virtues. It can serve the purpose of human suppression and tyranny far easier than democracy.

The only just and viable economic system for modern man would be one that would not only equitably serve the greatest majority of the people as possible, but would also reward virtue more than vice. Modern science and technology has given man the tools to achieve the purpose but not the morality.

The economy stupid and education stupid have done nothing much to improve the moral image of modern man.

Modern science and technology, without morality; nationalism, religion, competition, and winning at all costs, and the speed, greed, prejudice, crime, and violence of runaway capitalism keep man marching steadily backward rather than forward.

There is no greater fool than an overeducated fool. Too much education, so badly used, with a mass media so decided to moronic sensationalism and meaningless triviality, emanating from an overloaded store of questionable information, broadcasted too easily over the Internet, help make up modern man's new Dante's *Inferno*.

The founding fathers of the United States were mostly prudent and cautious men—frugal and pragmatic. They were weary and apprehensive that the nation's industrial and economic development would go too fast, and ruin all the aspirations of humanism, idealism, and democracy. Human progress was infinitely more important to them than the speed and greed of the fast developing science, technology, and commerce.

The modern American politicians, knowing full well the idealistic and progressive intentions of their nation's founding fathers, have constantly chosen to trade away human progress for the speed and greed of military and commercial imperialism.

While some other nations work hard for human progress, and discount any political celebrity cult in favor of developing better and more efficient government, the United States of American becomes bogged down in the political demagoguery of its antiquated and wasteful two major political party system.

While other nations progress to achieve a more representative government for their people, the United States regresses with a government of too many millionaires and political demagogues not representative enough of the vast majority of its people. The result is that the United States finds itself the most backward of the advanced rich nations of the world, in the health, education, and social care of their people.

To make matters worse, a jealous imperialistic American government tries to intimidate other nations into lowering their higher standards of caring for their people. This lunatic and cruel American government dictate is the direct legacy of Ronald Reagan, who was so corrupt that he destroyed most of the American people's trust in government.

Without enough trust in government the American people have become addicted to an immature all-out hatred of any government. Anarchy and senseless violence have risen with a new phenomenon, not seen in years in the supposedly civilized nation, namely the rising number of armed militias. Some call this tragic development, another one of former President Reagan's legacies.

Nothing could be more harmful and irresponsible for the United States than to allow a handful of power hungry demagogues in Congress, with the false economic priorities of speed and greed, to dismantle the already lagging social security net of the nation.

As social injustice and economic inequality rise in the United States, so does domestic crime and violence. If social problems rise too much because of government's lack of interest in solving them, the whole domestic and international military security of the nation crumbles.

The Evil American Empire

Not long ago, some courageous American public servants, not yet addicted to the pursuit of power and wealth, banded together to pass the nation's social security act. Fifty years later a new type of public servant, completely addicted to the pursuit of wealth and power, attack their own people's social security system with a vengeance.

The new image of the American president or public servant, or even the ordinary businessman, is completely different in a most unflattering way. Social responsibility has been completely thrown away.

Bill Gates, a supposedly brilliant man and Chairman of Microsoft, seemed completely befuddled during an interview when a reporter asked him about his views on social responsibility. He fumbled worse than a three-year-old.

The new American image of man is the old image rejected as the ugly American—a loud-mouthed bragger without conscience or social responsibility, dedicated to materialism, the profit motive, the lust for power, and self-indulgence.

To the regret of the vast majority of the American people, they never received the peace dividend after Chernobyl and the fall of the Soviet Empire that their Cold War Hawk leadership had promised them for so long.

Instead, the American people are asked for more and more sacrifices by a leadership whose own self-indulgence has become legendary. The rate of increased earnings for chief corporate managers has exploded from 40 times the average worker in 1970 to 225 times the average worker in 1990. Politicians in high places in the United States buy more than merit their offices.

The United States is so lucky that its people are so passive and protest government folly much less than in most other normal democracies. The reason the people in the U.S. don't protest as much as other countries is because of its huge size, the growing arrogance and isolation of the nation's leadership, and the loss of all hope of the American Dream.

History lies continuously, and man lives with his delusions. Unbridled capitalism has never worked very well for the majority of the people in any democracy. One has to take a backseat to the other, and it is nearly always democracy that loses. Corporate capitalism is a natural enemy to democratic individual free enterprise capitalism.

Free markets have, of course, never existed. Soviet-style communism was nothing more than an insane, poorly-managed form of centralized capitalism.

Modern man is a very materialistic and economically wasteful entity. His speed and greed produce his dismal image of a man, completely out of control, steeped in self-gratification, opulence, crime, violence, and all around human misery.

The backward pace of man accelerates as the irresponsible wealth, greed, and consumption of his economic system grows. The beneficiaries are all those who have a sick love of power and who are anxious to destroy humanism and individualism.

Incredibly, the new image of modern man, lusting over his newest computer and thinking up his next greed, appears to be a man, more vulnerable as an individual than ever before in history.

As modern man becomes more and more physically sedentary and incapable, he becomes more mentally and intellectually absurd.

The two major American political party conventions only show off the nation's growing political corruption and decline. Thanks to modern technology and the mass media, the American people are told that the avowed platforms of these conventions are nothing more than false image making and imaginative lying.

With all the American politicians admitting that the nation is declining faster than they can invent their newest witch doctor remedies, it is a wonder of the world that any American would want to shake hands with any of the nation's most famous politicians. It is only the nation's mass media, with its unremitting profit motive that desperately ignores reality and invents the little remaining credibility in the American political system.

The proof of all of this is the growing sentiment of the vast majority of the American people that neither of their two major political parties has any interest at all in a more honest and efficient government.

Just one example of this growing American government folly is the mayhem and chaos in the nation's airports, sixteen years after the weak minded President Reagan fired all the nation's air traffic controllers. They were never replaced in adequate enough numbers to protect the flying public's interests.

In walking backward so steadily, modern man creates his own danger and misery. In the United States, not only has he cut the average family of four standard of living in half in the past 40 years, but his welfare program for the already rich keeps on escalating.

The coddling of the rich by the American political establishment has become completely scandalous. Dishonorable political donations, right in the White House itself, have destroyed the credibility of both the nation's president and vice president.

A man as corrupt as the former representative Dan Rosentenkoski of Illinois, who pleaded guilty to several counts of fraud, was able to strut openly in the halls of Congress for 36 years, was admired and even revered by the American political establishment. Rostenkoski was even allowed to keep his spectacular public service pension.

Truly, by the time of Bill Clinton's presidency, the American political establishment had lost all credibility of honesty and integrity. The nation was stepping backward into the old anarchy of the robber barons, no longer single individuals, but now chief executive officers of the corporate world, controlling and extorting every aspect of the nation's economy.

Clearly, the American economy was the best controlled economy man has ever devised to favor the rich over the middle class and the poor.

Nothing could be more ominous for predicting the American economy's future than viewing the wasteful billion dollar outer space program. In one example, the United States, France, and Russia cooperated on the same project, wasting hundreds of millions of dollars. A desperately poor Russia was selling its advanced rocket technology to the rich nations of the United States and France to gain the hard currency needed to slaughter insurgents on its evaporating borders.

All three nations were among the biggest armament sellers around the world. All were guilty of the slaughter of innocent foreign people with the forfeiture of their national honor.

Modern man admits that he has built nuclear weapons and power plants that could blow up in his face, just like in Chernobyl in the former Soviet Empire. Nevertheless, modern man continues to encourage unlimited greed, consumption, and economic development that kills countless varieties of life forms, and harms his own health, as well as the health of his environment.

Where once the native American living philosophy was one of pragmatism, simplicity, quality, and frugality, it has become an extravagant love of consumption, power, speed, and greed. The new American system encourages young people to rely more and more on credit, making the new generations of Americans the most debt ridden in the nation's history.

Small wonder that the ugly American has resurfaced all around the world, selling weapons and merchandise instead of promoting good will, peace, democracy, and disarmament. This ugly American always acts so surprised at the growing hunger and homelessness of the poor and the slaughter of the innocent at home and abroad that his own false priorities have helped cause.

As dumb as most lower animals are supposed to be, not many would willingly choose as lunatic a quality of life and style of life as modern man has chosen. History lies, man and his leadership have always been his own worst enemy. Modern man has absolutely no justifiable claim of being any more intelligent than in his tragic past. The more man becomes enamored with his modern science and technology, his DNA, and his new abilities at cloning, the more he appears intellectually idiotic.

The startling new advances in science and technology have made modern man more backward, especially in his economic and political freedom and independence. This also means that modern man is losing ground intellectually.

The super computer and its artificial intelligence produces speed, efficiency, and a great deal of uniformity which are all potential enemies to democracy, humanism, and individualism. Computers and their automated abilities trivialize work, intellect, individualism, and creativity much more than they inspire true quality and art. Nothing is more ominous to true future human individual creativity and variety.

Modern man's overeducated fools, politicians, economists, hoarders, and great egotists who form most of his visible leadership, turn around against him to become his worst enemies.

The evil American empire is so extensive only because the United States appears to be, at this time in history, modern man's last remaining true superpower.

Fortunately for the American people, considered throughout the world as the most generous people in the world, probably because they are the best integrated and the wealthiest, the visible

American leadership has never been the real American people's leadership.

The great dunces in the White House are free to come and go, but somewhere among the American people, the true leaders of political freedom, democracy, and all around fraternity are keeping a very wary eye upon them.